Has it ever occurred to you how many artifacts are produced with a right-handed bias? If you are right-handed, you may never have noticed. If you are left-handed, however, you most certainly will have. The bias in favour of right-handedness runs right through society. *The Left-Handed Book* suggests some ways in which to redress the balance, and argues that left-handedness is not a handicap and never has been.

Both Simon Langford and Ed McLachlan are left-handed.

SIMON LANGFORD

The Left-Handed Book

with illustrations by McLachlan

GRAFTON BOOKS

A Division of the Collins Publishing Group

LONDON GLASGOW
TORONTO SYDNEY AUCKLAND

Grafton Books
A Division of the Collins Publishing Group
8 Grafton Street, London W1X 3LA

A Grafton Paperback Original 1984
Reprinted 1987

ISBN 0-586-06078-2

Printed and bound in Great Britain by
Collins, Glasgow

Set in Times

Contents

Introduction

Carl Philip Emmanuel Bach, Rex Harrison, Billy the Kid, Babe Ruth, Olivia de Havilland, the Emperor Tiberius, Danny Kaye, Mandy Rice-Davies, Jack the Ripper, Cole Porter, Charlie Chaplin, Judy Garland, George VI – not the most obvious company to be grouped together, you might think, but they share a feature that sets them apart from possibly 90 per cent or slightly less of mankind – they all were, or are, left-handed.

In a world dominated by dextrals (right-handers), left-handers (sinistrals) have always had a rough deal. Religious taboo, social stigma, primitive superstition and a general dislike of the unusual or unfamiliar have branded left-handers, at best, as mildly unfortunate, and, at worst, as social outcasts. Traces of this past prejudice still survive – if only in thoughtlessness and a lack of imagination – as I hope this book shows.

As well as providing a survey of some of the thinking there has been about left-handedness (and there has been no shortage of that since the time of Plato and no doubt earlier) this book hopes to be of some practical help to left-handers, their parents and teachers. It suggests ways of approaching what is a perfectly common phenomenon when stripped of the mystery and misunderstanding that has surrounded it for so long. And in the final section it lists a range of left-handed equipment which can transform needlessly awkward daily tasks into ones that any left-hander will find as easy to approach as right-handers. Not that we should be complacent. Take a look at the watch you're wearing now and consider how awkward it is for a left-hander to alter the hands or wind it (if that mundane task is still necessary in this quartz-timed age). No, there is still some way to go, and I hope that this book will indicate some of the directions in which we should move.

Left-handedness is not a handicap and never has been. It is only the workings of a right-handed world that have made it appear so. If there is any difference between the two hands it is largely a mechanical one that can soon be overcome.

Many have worked in this important field before and many are active in it at present. In particular I would like to acknowledge the invaluable work of Michael Barsley and Peter Broom of Anything Left Handed Ltd., in promoting the cause of the left-hander today.

Keep left.

S.L.

CHAPTER 1

In the Beginning . . .

'Sickle. A very sharp and handy tool from Germany. 15". Fully LH', reads the catalogue of *Anything Left Handed Limited* in London, for the past dozen years or so the world's leading centre for the retailing of left-handed implements and appliances – but more of that presently. For the moment let us concentrate on the sickle.

What does the catalogue tell us? That the implement is a 'sickle' (raising a flicker of archaeological interest at the outset); that it is a serviceable tool; that it is made in Germany (implying that you won't trip over heaps of similar articles in garden centres and hardware shops around the world); and most importantly that it is left-handed. You may argue that the ready access of powered strimmers and mowers has forced the lowly sickle into retirement, but the fact remains that for the left-handed gardener a sickle specifically designed for his dominant hand is still something of a novelty. And this has been the case since the sickle was first cast way back in the Bronze Age.

We owe this access of intelligence to Paul Sarasin, a French archaeologist who specialized in man's early implements. From finds made in Spain, Switzerland, Southern France, Africa and Scandinavia he noticed that some Neolithic tools were sharpened on the left side and others on the right. From this he concluded that whoever made these stone 'knives' or hatchets felt no need to conform to one pattern of use. The tools revealed an almost equal division between right- and left-handedness. Stone Age man, it appeared, didn't really care which hand he used. It was only when he moved up a league and started manufacturing sophisticated tools, like the sickle, that right-handedness started to assert itself.

If we stop to consider the time and trouble that must have been spent making a sickle at that time it stands to reason that the craftsman would take equal care in targeting his wares at the largest market sector. It is this fact that leads many anthropologists and their like to mark this as the beginning of our right-handed world.

Looking further back into prehistory many experts argue that cave drawings of animals even imply a left-handed dominance in early man. The reasoning goes like this: the further back you look, the more animals there are drawn in their right profile; these animals must by force of circumstances have been drawn from memory – no one could have made a life study from the deep recesses of a cave; it's unlikely that they were always seen facing to the right; therefore their right profile on the cave wall must have resulted from the artist's own thinking process, which saw and painted with a left-handed bias. By the same token the animals drawn in left profile must have been created by a similar process. As the number of right profile and left profile drawings balanced out, the argument goes, the movement from a left-handed dominance to an ambidextrous state must have occasioned it. Coupled with the evidence from stone tools, this backs up the belief that our Stone Age forefathers were fairly easy-going when it came to deciding which hand they were going to use. In that case why should the right hand have achieved supremacy from the Bronze Age onwards?

On a practical level the answer is reasonably straightforward. By concentrating on the use of only one hand, training is simplified and faster than trying to cope with teaching the use of both (as thousands of left-handed writers know to their cost). Constant use of the same hand naturally leads to improved skill and strength. And these in turn promote improved efficiency, endurance and (literally in this case) dexterity. The arguments for opting for the dominant use of one hand have a lot going for them.

Then there are the social considerations. The leader of a primitive group is quite likely to be the one who excels in the use of tools and by analogy weapons. As a leader he will naturally seek to impose his will on his followers who, if they have any sense, will fall into line without complaint. Minority groups have seldom had an easy passage and left-handers in a right-handed prehistoric society were probably only too aware of their difference. They conformed, just as left-handed gardeners and farm workers since have conformed by clumsily adapting to sickles designed to serve the majority.

This is of course a gross simplification of an infinitely more complex issue, and one that fails to take into account the crucial question as to why dextrals got the upper hand in the first place. All the same, it does illustrate how social, economic and military conditioning may have influenced the development of handedness from the mid-morning of civilization.

CHAPTER 2

Nature versus Nurture

When it comes to explaining the origins of handedness one guess is very nearly as good as another. From Plato to the present, theories have been voiced and almost as quickly stifled; though as befits a bi-lateral subject, they fall into two broad categories. There are those that seek to explain the dominance of one hand over the other in terms of environment, education, upbringing and similar external forces, on the one hand. While on the other are ranked those that prefer to look deep inside our very being to find the cause of our laterality in a birthright transmitted from our ancestors.

One school of thought puts its money on the sun, or to be more accurate on sun-worship. This may not appear to have that much to do with our hands but it is all-important in the development of man's sense of direction. From direction there followed an awareness of sidedness, which in terms of the human frame led naturally to a partiality for things connected with one half of the body – and this happened to be the right.

For anyone living in the northern hemisphere, which has always included the great majority of mankind, tracking the sun's progress across the sky has meant facing south, and in order to follow its passage across the heavens the watcher must constantly turn to the right until the sun sinks and dies in the west.

It doesn't require a huge leap of the imagination to extend this into the realm of primitive religion. The sun was a source of wonder and fear; the origin of life itself. It brought warmth and light. It instituted order in the seasons and the daily routine of work and sleep. With its growing vigour in the spring it gave promise of food for the coming year and rich harvests in the autumn. Sun worship represents man's earliest foray into religion and vestiges of it survive in folklore and superstition all over the world. These in their turn have often become inter-woven with other taboos associated with the left hand.

The actual movement of the sun towards the right has become more institutionalized. Clocks follow the same course, as might be expected; most children's games are played in this direction; and compass navigation moves through its 360 degrees in the same way. Not unreason-ably, moving in the opposite direction, or 'widdershins' (from the old German words 'wider' – against – and 'sin' – 'course', or 'journey'), has always courted disaster, as we'll discover later. So, taken all in all, anything that moved towards or favoured the right was acceptable and desirable; anything that swung towards the left was re-garded with suspicion and in some cases trepidation. That at least is the line of thought followed by the sun-worship lobby.

Plato took a more level-headed approach, as one might expect. He blamed careless nannies and nursing mothers. 'In the use of the hand we are, as it were, maimed by the folly of our nurses and mothers', he wrote in Book VII of his *Laws*, 'for although our several limbs are by nature balanced, we create a difference in them by habit.' He also held that the arm that cradles the baby governs the child's future handedness. Consider for a moment the little one clutched by its mother as she tries to soothe it while answering a knock at the door or choosing her shopping from a supermarket shelf. If she is right-handed, as the majority of women are (the majority of left-handers being men), she is almost certain to hold the baby in her left arm to make full use of her right hand. In this position the child is held tight against its mother with its right arm totally immobilized, leaving the left hand to make every tactile contact with the rest of mankind and the world at large. (This naturally begs the question, why aren't there more left-handers in that case? And so deflates the argument.)

The primitive warfare theory argues that primitive man soon realized that the beating he could feel in his chest played no small part in staying alive. When the beating stopped life came to an abrupt halt. Since the beating appears to come from the left side of the chest, proponents claimed, primitive man felt a need to guard this area of his body, and the left hand was the most obvious means of carrying a rock or whatever form of shield took his fancy. This left the right hand as the principal means of attack. At the same time it was also nearest an opponent's heart in hand-to-hand combat and so had the more favourable access to this when it came to striking a winning blow. Thus the right hand became the aggressive, active hand and the left was relegated to the role of passive defender.

That awe-inspiring Scottish scholar, Thomas Carlyle, was one of the leading advocates of this line of argument, though it has to be admitted that even his reasoning came almost as an afterthought, as his journal entry for 15 June 1871 shows:

It is curious to consider the institution of the Right hand among universal mankind; probably the very oldest human institution that exists, indispensable to all human cooperation whatsoever. He that has seen three mowers, one of whom is left-handed, trying to work together, and how impossible it is, has witnessed the simplest form of an impossibility, which but for the distinction of a 'right hand' would have pervaded all human beings . . . Why that particular hand was chosen is a question not to be settled, not worth asking except as a kind of riddle; probably arose in fighting; most important to protect your heart and its adjacencies, and to carry the shield in that hand.

The primitive warfare theory had a respectable following even centuries after anatomical investigation had shown that the human heart is more or less central in the body and only appears to beat on the left. Carlyle had evidently overlooked this minor detail.

Stone Age combat had a part to play in another popular theory that held sway for some time in the last century. This time the emphasis was on the hand that went to pick up a weapon; the assumption being that both hands were available at that time, neither being hampered by a shield. Sir John Struthers, another 19th century Scot who applied his mind to the problem, concluded that in the early days of armed attack our ancestors probably picked up any convenient weapon that was lying about, such as a rock or fallen branch. In bending down to reach this, Palaeolithic man would have leant to the right since, according to Struthers and others who thought along the same lines, the distribution of his organs placed his centre of gravity to the right of centre. Therefore his right hand would have been the one to pick up the weapon, or anything else for that matter, and consequently the same hand would have been the one to use it.

Struthers was one of the many respected students of handedness who backed the theory of visceral distribution (as this displacement of the internal organs is termed). His fellow countryman, and Professor of Physiology at Glasgow University, Alexander Buchanan, added his weight to the idea by concentrating on the mechanical advantages of right-handedness, as he saw them.

He suggested that since the centre of gravity in most people lies slightly to the right we balance more effectively on the left foot. This leads to us becoming right-footed and in consequence right-handed.

The snag with this school of thought is that it doesn't give a convincing account of the origins of left-handedness. Buchanan tried to argue that this was brought about by an opposite centre of gravity, one that veered to the left of centre in other words. He failed to give evidence to prove this point, nor did he adequately explain why it should have occurred in the first place. Perhaps he might have altered his views if he had paid close attention to the work of Sir Thomas Browne, who devoted a significant portion of his *Vulgar Errors* to left-handedness a couple of centuries earlier.

Written in 1648, this masterpiece of deflation explodes many fallacies then current, and in lingering for some time on the subject of handedness becomes one of the first serious studies of the subject since ancient times.

Browne was one of the first to dismiss the idea that the right hand became dominant as a sole result of the need for the left hand to protect the heart. His reasoning was that the heart isn't on the left of the body any more than it is on the right, as we have already noted. He applied the same anatomical logic to visceral distribution, which became the cornerstone of the centre of gravity theories, commenting:

> For the seat of the heart and liver in one side, whereby men become left-handed, it happeneth too rarely to countenance an effect so common; for the seat of the liver on the left is monstrous, and rarely to be met with in the observations of physicians.

He goes on to mention that left-handers and right-handers have been found in whom the position of the liver is at variance with the strong emphasis placed on its location in this theory. He ends with the most damning note of all. Our ape friends and erstwhile cousins, whose livers are defiantly on the right, show no distinctive preference for one hand or the other. In that case why should the location of our livers have any influence on our own manual partiality? Why indeed?

Where Buchanan and his followers argued that handedness could be explained by the dominance of one foot over the other, the 19th century American researcher, Beaufort Sims Parson, attempted to explain handedness in terms of eye dominance. He actually set out nine possible origins ranging from uneven blood supply to the brain, to habit and upbringing, but he spent most of his study concentrating on the link between the dominant eye and the chosen hand.

He set out to prove that vision has a greater impact on our lives than any other stimulus. In particular he argued that as babies almost all our voluntary movements depend on vision. If he was right, and few think he was, the implication would be that those of us with dominant left eyes would be left-handed and vice versa. Parson argued that what he termed 'certain dominant single faculties', speech and memory for example, originate in the same half of the brain that control handedness and eyedness. This led him to suggest that this link led to the most direct and fastest co-ordination of vision with 'intellect, will and action'.

Similar ideas are found in the theories of cerebral dominance which have been current in recent years (we will come back to this), but as for Parson's principal thesis that the dominant eye leads the dominant hand, the evidence is stacked against him. For one thing, the great number of people who have dominant hands and eyes on opposite sides suggests that his ideas and the facts may conflict, while surveys among the congenitally blind have shown the same proportion of left-handers to right-handers as that found among the sighted population. That isn't to say that eye dominance has no bearing on handedness; it may well be part of the complicated matrix, but it certainly isn't the one and only cause as claimed by advocates even more sold on the idea than Parson, one of whom, G. M. Gould, wrote in 1908:

> Thus vision is the father of action, of right-handed action, and right-eyedness is bound up as a precedent, synchronous, and causal factor of right-handedness.

Claims like that have been damped down in the intervening seventy-five years. For one thing the definition of eye dominance has been argued over extensively.

In the first studies it was assumed that the dominant eye was the one with better sight. However, later research indicated that this wasn't always the case. In fact, in one study made in 1933 results showed that only 50 per cent of those tested showed a preference for the eye with greatest visual acuity. Over the years a variety of tests have been developed to establish eye preference which are of obvious value as far as eyesight is concerned but probably have little direct bearing on determining the origins of handedness.

The one area of experience in which eye dominance and left-handedness run parallel is education. Here children with a preference for the eye with weaker sight occasionally have difficulty with reading, while the difficulties encountered by left-handed children in the classroom are legion. They can't use scissors used by their right-handed friends to cut out paper shapes; they often have a terrible time trying to write; and several reading problems have been connected with left-handed children, in particular forms of dyslexia.

Those who champion the theory that education is the cause of handedness claim that only a very few people are naturally strongly left-handed or strongly right-handed. According to them, right-handedness comes as a direct result of education. At the head of this body of thought is Sir Daniel Wilson (yet another Scot) who reached the pinnacle of his academic career a century ago by being elected President of Toronto University.

Unlike many authorities who investigated left-handedness, Wilson could draw on his own experience as a sinistral; though he later became an accomplished ambidextral and taught himself to write with his right hand. In 1872 he wrote a long essay on the subject that claimed in its opening:

Man converts one hand into the special organ servant of his will; while the other is relegated to a subordinate place, as its mere aider and supplementer.

His study ranged far and wide, from ancient Egyptian tombs where he noted that Rameses is depicted in battle setting about his foes with a club grasped in his left hand, to the icy wastes of the Arctic where he concluded that left-handedness was rare among Eskimoes after hearing of one hunter's surprise at seeing a polar bear throwing a lump of ice at a walrus with its left paw.

In the final analysis he comes down on the side of education as the prime cause of right-handed domination:

> In every sudden and unpremeditated action, the prompt use of the left hand shows that there remains, after the utmost educational training, some inherent impulse, resulting in a greater aptitude in the one hand than the other. My own experience, being left-handed myself, shows the education of a lifetime contending with only partial success to overcome an instinctive natural preference.

The primary argument against this is that in all societies it can be proved that movement in handedness has always started towards the right. That said, it's not unreasonable to suppose that the proportion of those unflinchingly right-handed is fairly small, as seems to be the case with total left-handers. It may be education that conditions the majority of us to adopt the right hand as the dominant one. Had the swing been the other way, as many might have become left-handed according to the same argument.

The education theory adopts an impartial attitude to handedness, allowing that, but for a change of circumstances, the sinistrals might represent the majority. A far harsher analysis is found in the argument applied by Dr

Abram Blau, Professor of Psychiatry at the New York University College of Medicine, and his fellow theorists. They set out to establish right-handedness as the normal, well-ordered human response to the environment, balanced against which left-handedness was a perverse distortion cutting across the grain of social order.

In the course of his medical work, Blau came across many cases of mental and nervous disorders which he was able to relate to left-handedness. From his work he concluded that handedness had no basis in man's physiological make-up or in hereditary transmission. The right hand became dominant, he argues, because social conditioning made it so. Left-handedness arises therefore as a direct deviation from this norm, brought about by 'an inherent deficiency, faulty education, or emotional negativism'. Of the three he plumps for the last as the most common type of left-handedness; one that develops from a child's active resistance to environmental and social pressures to become right-handed, assuming that these exist and that the child has the capacity to acquire them should he so wish. In other words the development of left-handedness is a deliberate challenge to the otherwise natural and normal strain of right-handedness.

Cesare Lombroso, a 20th century Italian psychiatrist, went a stage further and looked on left-handedness as a sure sign of a degenerate, quoting the higher proportion of left-handers found among criminals and the mentally deranged. Blau is rather less extreme in his thesis, preferring to look on left-handedness in the same light as the wilful behaviour of a truculent child. He linked this with the broader field of infantile rejection, which in many cases stems from a denial of maternal affection, and concluded that much left-handedness could be laid at the door of an emotionally deprived home. At one stage he even suggests that this negative attitude takes the extreme form of refusing to obey calls of nature. Left-handed infants are not just cussed, they may even, according to Blau's Theory, be constipated! (He has Freud to thank for that spark of inspiration.) With the dice so heavily loaded against left-handedness in the form of social and religious taboos, not to mention the many practical difficulties that constitute a ceaseless pattern of minor frustrations in everyday life, Blau wonders why a small proportion of mankind doggedly stick to using the wrong hand, as he views it. This underlines his principal contention that handedness is a result of 'nurture' not 'nature'.

Blau's ideas conflict drastically with the theories of those who supported the view that handedness is transmitted from parents to their children. This hereditary explanation achieved its greatest popularity around the turn of the century, encouraged no doubt by the publication of Mendel's findings among the pea vines of his monastery garden. The Austrian monk had carried out a series of meticulous studies with some 10,000 sweet pea plants, and his findings came to form the basis of modern genetics. From the careful analysis of the offspring of plants showing different characteristics (some might have had green seeds, for instance, some yellow) Mendel was able to establish that these characteristics are governed by genetic factors passed from one generation to the next. These might be either 'dominant' characteristics, ones in which the offspring displayed a particular uniformity, where the parents had a marked difference, or 'recessive' ones. In the course of his work, though, Mendel proved that the two never blended, so making it possible for an individual with a dominant characteristic to carry the genetic make-up for a recessive characteristic to the next generation without displaying it itself. Eight years before Men-

del's work was made public, Frank H. Crushing wrote in
The American Anthropologist:

> The hand of man has been so intimately associated with
> the mind of man that it has moulded intangible thoughts
> no less than the tangible products of his brain. So intimate
> was this association during the very early period of man's
> mental growth that it may be affirmed to be, like so many
> other hereditary traits, still dominantly existent in the
> hands of all of us.

He was followed by a number of researchers who latched
on to the Mendelian *ratio* seeking to explain the right-
hander as the dominant element and the left-hander as
the recessive in Mendel's law of heredity.

Other studies have been made of the incidence of left-
handedness in families in which both parents were left-
handed and those in which the parents were both right-
handed. The results showed that 50 per cent of the
children of left-handed parents will be left-handed too;
while only 2 per cent of the children of right-handed
parents will be left-handed.

One specific study of handedness was centred on the
Scottish Kerr family, which has been famous for centuries for the large number of its members who were left-
handed. Many of them built castles with anti-clockwise
spiral staircases that favoured left-handed swordsmen
when it came to defending them. They may well have
given rise to expressions such as 'Ker-handit' and
'carry-handed' which are traditional names for
left-handed people. In 1974 a survey of Kerrs showed
that there was a significantly greater number of left-
handed people bearing that name than there was in a
similar sample group without a family tradition of left-
handedness.

Among other explanations for handedness one of the most prominent, as mentioned earlier, has been the theory of cerebral dominance, in which it is suggested that there may be a connection between the relationship of the two hemispheres of the brain and either right- or left-handedness. Again, Sir Thomas Browne was among the front-runners with this claim, though it was another two hundred years before any concrete proof appeared. In 1861 the Royal Society published a weight table for every part of the human anatomy which showed that in most cases the left hemisphere of the brain, the one that governs the right side of the body, was the heavier. This seemed to support the idea that the dominant half of the brain conditioned the dominant side of the body, as manifested in handedness, eyedness and footedness.

Sir Daniel Wilson took a lively interest in this work and waited eagerly for a suitable left-handed specimen to come his way to test the theory for himself. He even offered his own brain to fellow scientists for research after his death, before the opportunity he had been waiting for arrived in the nick of time. An old soldier whose left-handedness had caused no end of problems in the army died in the Toronto Provincial Asylum. Wilson was invited to attend the autopsy at which the man's brain was removed and the two hemispheres weighed. Wilson naturally hoped that the right one was the heavier, and when their weights were compared he had the pleasure of seeing this confirmed.

Later authorities, notably Dr D. J. Cunningham in 1902, developed this theme, though most sought a more substantial and less arbitrary answer to the matter than Wilson, whose proof seemed altogether too simple. Cunningham believed firmly that handedness was hereditary and stated in a famous Huxley Memorial Lecture that

'Right-handedness is due to a transmitted functional pre-eminence of the left brain'.

His ideas tie in with others put forward by later researchers, especially those concerned with the study of the relationship between the brain and language. If we look at other animals we find that most species show a balanced preference between left-paw dominance and right-paw dominance, quite unlike man's very obvious preference for the right hand. Animals have a very limited language capacity and in most cases virtually none at all. Man on the other hand has a highly developed speech capability. Could there be any connection here?

The answer is that there might well be. Although the two halves of our brains are almost symmetrical they appear to have different roles and house different faculties. The left hemisphere (the one that controls the right side of the body) has been shown to be the one that also houses the speech faculty in 90–99 per cent of right-handers and 50–70 per cent of left-handers and ambidextrals. Studies of brain-damaged patients have also shown that those who lose the use of the right hemisphere of their brains also lose the ability to remember music and faces and have difficulty in performing a number of tasks that do not involve speech. In the case of those who lose the use of their left hemisphere, one of the most notable features is their resultant loss of speech.

Other surveys have shown that the left hemisphere seems better equipped to deal with logical progression, working with figures and organizing information than the right hemisphere. This side of the brain appears to control our spatial awareness, our ability to make aesthetic and artistic judgments, and the way we recognize faces and other non-verbal stimuli.

There are cases of left-handers who sustain damage to their left hemisphere without any perceptible loss of speech, the implication here being that their speech faculty resides in the right hemisphere. It must be said that cases like these represent only a small minority of the population. Even so, they point to a general conclusion that speech and handedness are connected, and this poses the chicken and egg question 'Which came first?'

As yet there is no firm evidence one way or the other. Some researchers argue that man's apparent bias to the right, however small, led our ancestors to use the right hand paramountly when communicating by gestures. As these gave way to a more sophisticated form of communication that led ultimately to speech, the left hemisphere of the brain, which had been controlling the gestures all along, naturally took over the rôle of governing this radically new form of conveying ideas and information.

Those who believe that speech was rooted in the left hemisphere of the brain before right-handedness point to the delicate and intricate movements common to both the hands and the vocal cords. With the left side of the brain apparently best equipped to deal with such precise and complex operations, was it not better suited to take over the equally intricate speech processes?

A final possibility under consideration for the origin of braindedness and handedness is that of a genetic basis. Some believe that handedness is as much a matter of chance as tossing a coin, the difference being that one side of the coin has the advantage of a genetic bias (in favour of the left side of the brain and consequently the right hand). If the coin comes down on the unbiased side a left-handed baby is the result.

Further evidence comes from studies of left-handers themselves, and shows that those who come from a long line of sinistrals usually possess some language faculty in both halves of the brain; this has sometimes enabled brain-damaged patients to maintain some speech facility, whereas those left-handers who have come from a family with no sinistral history frequently lose all power of speech after sustaining damage to the left hemisphere, suggesting that their language faculties are located solely in that half of the brain, as with right-handers. Why should those from a left-handed background have a different brain arrangement to those from a right-handed background? The chances of any exterior forces like education being responsible seem remote and in the face of other evidence a genetic basis seems the most reasonable answer.

For the time being no one has come up with a concrete explanation for the origins of handedness. Perhaps no one ever will. Today we do at least have a broader canvas on which to work, but we still haven't been able to efface totally the superstitions and taboos that have become ingrained in so many cultures and that have caused left-handedness to be regarded with suspicion and dread from time immemorial.

CHAPTER 3

The Sheep and the Goats

With only a few exceptions religion and worship throughout the history of the world have been defiantly right-
handed. A quick look at Christianity confirms this. The
blessing is given and the sign of the cross are made with the
right hand. At Holy Communion the bread and wine,
symbolizing the very essence of Christianity, are passed to
the communicants from left to right and they in turn receive
the bread in their right hands supported by the left and take
the chalice with the right hand uppermost. In this most
sacred of rituals the left hand is merely employed as a
supporter; the right is the hand of grace.

In many pictures of the Last Judgment Christ if depicted
with his right hand raised toward heaven, pointing the way
to eternal life, while his left hand points downwards to the
eternal damnation and everlasting flames of hell. On the
cross the penitent thief hangs on his right side. And in
telling his followers 'I am the Light of the World', Christ
confers his own divinity on the symbol of the sun, which
had been and still was the focal point in its own right for
many other religions. Traces of sun, or clockwise, movement survive too in many Christian communities. It was
once common for coffins to be walked three times round a
church in this direction before being lowered into a grave,
and many Scottish weddings ended with a ritual clockwise
procession round the church for the same reason.

Christianity comes in for closer scrutiny in a moment but
sun worship, touched on briefly already, deserves further
exploration.

In Japan the sun was worshipped as a living deity and faithful followers would trek up to the summit of Mount Fuji to pray to the first rays of sunlight that appeared above the horizon. (In Oxford they sing a hymn in the same way once a year on May morning.) In fact the sun became so popular in Japan that the royal family decided to cash in on this and claimed its descent from a sun goddess, Amaterasu.

On the other side of the world the Incas were constructing elaborate sun temples facing eastwards where religious ceremonies were also performed at the first light of dawn. They too of course were ruled over by a king who also claimed to be directly descended from the sun.

In spite of the controversy that surrounds its actual purpose it seems likely that Stonehenge was probably used in some way for sun worship, and crowds of druids and less exotic devotees still gather there on May morning to watch the sun rise directly above the stone called the Friar's Heel and see it momentarily bathing the so-called Slaughter Stone in its blood-red light.

Come midsummer the Plains Indians of North America gathered in tribes in vast summer camps to perform their celebrated Sun Dances. In spite of their beguiling name, which conjures up images of children skipping round maypoles on village greens or doing something pretty and creative with hooped garlands, these were a thoroughly gruesome spectacle. For four days and nights the braves danced round the trunk of a cottonwood tree set up in the centre of a specially constructed enclosure, performing ritual gestures. There was no food, no drink and no rest, and to shatter the idea that this was in any sense four days of non-stop fun and games many of the dancers stuck wooden skewers through their pectoral muscles which were in turn attached to ropes tied to the pole in the middle; they danced round and round until the skewers were finally ripped from their flesh. They did this as a way of persuading the sun to favour them with good harvests and successful buffalo hunts, and it wasn't until 1904 that the government in Washington decided to promote their welfare in a less extreme manner and banned the Sun Dances. The ones that entertain tourists today are pale imitations of the real thing.

Among the sun gods of the Middle East, the birthplace of Christianity, were the Persian god Mithras, who developed such a strong following among Roman soldiers; Ra, the Egyptian god whose name was incorporated in the title Pharaoh, meaning 'Son of the Sun God'; Baal, who was worshipped by the Assyrians and who influenced the development of sun worship throughout the area; the Greek god Apollo; and the father of the gods of the Greek pantheon, Zeus.

Apart from the favoured direction of the sun's movement towards the right, direct right-handedness in these sun religions and their related mythologies is striking. Zeus held his bolts of lightning in his right hand and Clotho, one of the Fates, held the threads of life in hers. Moving further back in Greek mythology we find one clear reason for the rough justice meted out to the left hand from earliest times. This is the story of the castration of Uranus.

According to the myth, as related by Robert Graves, Uranus (a personification of Heaven) and Mother Earth gave birth to seven sons known as the Titans, the youngest of whom was Cronus. Uranus banished his boys to Tartarus, a particularly dingy part of the Underworld, and upset their mother greatly. So beside herself was the lady that she egged her sons on to attack their father. She gave Cronus a flint sickle and he led the other six in an attack on their father in his sleep. Uranus never stood a chance. Before he had had time to come to, Cronus was at his manhood and had castrated him, wielding the sickle in his right hand and (this is the crucial part) holding his father's genitals in his left, before casting them into the sea. The left hand has been suffering ever since and in few places more so than in the pages of the *Holy Bible*.

One count reveals over a hundred favourable references to the right hand in the scriptures and about a quarter as many unfavourable references to the left. The greatest concentration of 'right hand' quotations come from the Book of Psalms, of which these are a few examples:

> I have set the Lord always before me: because he is at my right hand, I shall not be moved.   *Psalm 16 v.8*

> Thou wilt shew me the path of life: in thy presence is fulness of joy; at thy right hand there are pleasures for evermore.
>   *Psalm 16 v.11*

> Let thy hand be upon the man of thy right hand, upon the son of man whom thou madest strong for thyself.
>   *Psalm 80 v.17*

> The voice of rejoicing and salvation is in the tabernacles of the righteous: the right hand of the Lord doeth valiantly.
> The right hand of the Lord is exalted; the right hand of the Lord doeth valiantly.   *Psalm 118 vv. 15 & 16*

Mentions of the left hand are notable in the Bible for their scarcity. The two most graphic cases are to be found in the *Book of Judges*. These deal specifically with the tribe of Benjamin whose name, just to confuse matters, means both 'Son of the South' and 'Son of the Right Hand'.

The first reference comes in Chapter 3, where the reader finds that '. . . the children of Israel served Eglon the king of Moab eighteen years'. The chronicler continues in the next verse (number 15):

But when the children of Israel cried unto the Lord, the Lord raised them up a deliverer. Ehud the son of Gera, a Benjamite, a man lefthanded: and by him the children of Israel sent a present unto Eglon the king of Moab.

He doesn't tell the reader what the present was but from what happened there's little doubt that Eglon would have happily gone without it. For his part Ehud made himself 'a dagger which had two edges, of a cubit length; and he did gird it under his raiment upon his right thigh'.

The Lord had chosen his man wisely. He knew the state of fear in which Eglon and most other kings lived at that time and the precautions they took to avoid assassination. All visitors were searched for hidden weapons, but in a dextral society few guards would think of searching for a weapon hidden for use by a left-handed man. If they frisked Ehud, they would have concentrated on his left thigh, where a right-hander would hide a dagger for easiest use. We can only assume that they didn't bother to examine his right thigh.

Anyhow the present was delivered and those that brought it were dismissed. Ehud now had to get the king on his own. He did this by telling Eglon that he had something secret to tell him. The servants were also sent off, leaving the two men alone in Eglon's 'summer parlour', as the translators of the King James's Bible quaintly call it. It was then that Ehud revealed that his message was from God, and saying this, he stood up, whipped out his dagger and plunged it into Eglon's bulging midriff. Now enters a touch of macabre farce. The author had previously mentioned that 'Eglon was a fat man', and this was confirmed as the dagger disappeared inside his voluminous folds of flab. Ehud kept his head, left the king sprawled dead on the floor, and locked the doors to give himself time, knowing that the guards would become suspicious if his private audience lasted too long, or if he departed without being seen off by the king in person.

His scheme worked perfectly. The guards 'tarried till they were ashamed', and only then went to fetch a key to see what was going on. By this time Ehud was scampering 'unto Seirath' as fast as he could. There he summoned the children of Israel as arranged and led them against the forces of Moab, massacring them to a man, a total of about 10,000. For the only known time in Biblical history God's left-hand man won the day!

The Benjamites as a tribe crop up a few chapters later in *Judges*, this time in a very unfavourable light. After what amounted to a case of gang rape in Gibeah which, as the author puts it, 'belongeth to Benjamin', the Levite whose concubine had been the victim cut her body into twelve pieces and sent these, as was the custom, throughout Israel as evidence of the vile crime committed in the town. This brutal assault galvanized the rest of the children of Israel into action against the Benjamites, and a force of 400,000 marched against them. The Benjamite force was greatly outnumbered, as the account in *Judges* 20 v.15 tells us:

> And the children of Benjamin were numbered at that time out of the cities twenty and six thousand men that drew sword.

However, they had one tactical advantage, or so it would appear from later casualty figures, because:

> Among all this people there were seven hundred chosen men lefthanded; every one could sling stones at an hair breadth, and not miss.

What effect this band of crack-shots had on the battle we are not told, but in the first encounter the Israelites were beaten back leaving 22,000 dead on the field, and in the second clash they again retreated, this time with 18,000 dead. Only after fasting for a day and making burnt offerings did the children of Israel obtain a promise of third time lucky from the Lord. They went out to battle the next day and slingers or no slingers sent the Benjamites packing, killing 25,000 in the process. And that would have been that for the tribe of Benjamin had not the risk of losing one of their tribes for ever persuaded the other children of Israel to provide them with a selection of virgins to restock the ranks.

Before leaving the Benjamites there is one other interesting point about this unpleasant business. The statistic on left-handedness given in the account in *Judges*, 26,000 right-handers to only 700 left-handers, is one of the earliest, if not the earliest, recorded. That said, it shows a significantly lower percentage of the population of Benjamin to be left-handed than is the case today. For our 1 in 10, or so, of the population who are left-handed, the Benjamites could only muster 1 in 37.

By far the most damning indictment of the left hand in the Bible is found in the *New Testament* in the parable of the sheep and the goats which comes towards the end of St Matthew's gospel, in the part known as the *Last Judgement*, which begins:

When the Son of man shall come again in his glory, and the holy angels with him, then shall he sit upon the throne of his glory:

And before him shall be gathered all nations: and he shall separate them one from another, as a shepherd divideth his sheep from the goats:

And he shall set the sheep on his right hand, but the goats on his left.

Then shall the King say unto them on his right hand, Come, ye blessed of my Father, inherit the kingdom prepared for you from the foundation of the world . . .

The goats on the other hand come in for rather different treatment:

Then shall he say unto them on the left hand, Depart from me, ye cursed, into everlasting fire, prepared for the devil and his angels . . .

And these shall go away into everlasting punishment: but the righteous into life eternal.

Any goat in the Middle East at that time had backed a loser, mind you. Goats were looked on as destructive, voracious creatures that ate anything in sight and ruined pasture in only a few seasons. The sheep was a very different beast. Its appetite was modest and controlled. It provided man with his principal source of meat and a fleece that could be spun into cloth to make clothes and tents, or just worn as a warm, if rather smelly, jacket. Link this with Christ, the Lamb of God, that took away the sins of the world, and the goat had little option but to join forces with the other side. The pagan god Pan, himself hoofed like the goat, was anathema to the fledgling religion, and the two were quickly amalgamated in Christian eyes to grow into the popular representation of the devil in the Middle Ages.

Since Christ, the Paschal Lamb, stood in the favoured position on the right of God the Father and since, as we have seen, both Jewish tradition as portrayed in the Old Testament and society in general favoured the right hand, Christianity rapidly developed strongly right-handed rituals.

Take marriage, for example. In the English-speaking world at least the bride stands on the groom's left, in the weaker, subservient position of the female. The wedding ring is placed on the third finger of her left hand, sometimes known as the 'heart finger' because of the belief that it has some special association with that organ. However, the wearing of rings on this finger is an ancient tradition that dates back to the ancient world. The Egyptians, Greeks and Romans all wore rings on this finger. The first were made of iron before this was replaced by gold. The ring was believed to be endowed with special powers that protected the wearer from the force of evil; some were engraved with magic inscriptions to add to their potency.

The importance attached to handedness in the wedding ceremony is seen in even sharper relief when compared with what the French call *mariage à main gauche*, or morganatic marriage in English. This last raised its head in public in 1936 when the British were plunged into the Mrs Simpson affair.

A morganatic marriage is one in which the husband weds a woman of lower social rank but one in which she is precluded from inheriting his property or, more importantly in the case of King Edward VIII and Mrs Simpson, rising to join him as an equal in rank and status. The same restrictions apply to any children they may have, as Horace Walpole wrote in 1788: 'The children of a left-handed alliance are not entitled to inherit.'

The tradition seems to have started in Germany where members of the aristocracy occasionally married beneath their station and confirmed the fact at the wedding ceremony where they offered their left hands to their brides in a gesture which in other circumstances was unquestionably one of shame. The term *morganatic* is derived from the German noun *Morgengabe*, which was the 'morning gift' presented by a husband to his wife the morning after consummation of their marriage which relieved him of any further liability. A greater snub to the left hand it would be hard to find! (Although almost as great a stigma is found in heraldry, where the Bend Sinister – what looks like a stripe running from top right-hand corner of a shield to the lower left edge – is a sign of bastardy.)

Turning to the world's other great religions we find an equal bias towards the right side. In Persian the expression 'to give the left' means to betray, and in the Jewish Talmud there is a reference to an arch betrayer, Samael, the Prince of Demons and Chief of Satans. In Hebrew the word 'Satan' means adversary, but Samael is related to the word for the left side, *se'mol*, and in the higher echelons of the angelic league Samael was placed on the left, opposite Michael who went to the favoured position on the right.

As part of the ritual for the Jewish Feast of Tabernacles the worshippers hold an *etrog* (a citrus fruit known as an 'Adam's apple') in their left hands while waving a palm branch to which is attached pieces of myrtle and willow in their right hands. While the palm branch, the *lulab*, is waved to the east, south, west and north, up, down, forwards and backwards, as an acknowledgment of God's universal and ubiquitous power and control, the fruit remains in the left hand as a possible reminder of the forbidden fruit in the Garden of Eden, with the left hand recalling Eve the transgressor – the inferior, female element who was herself created from a rib on Adam's left side.

Perhaps it is for this reason too that an absolute rejection of everything to do with the left was regarded as a sign of special divinity and blessedness. This was noted in particular in the lives of Christian saints, many of whom showed a strong antipathy for anything 'sinister' at a precociously early age. According to their biographers a lot of them refused to be suckled with the left breast!

Islam is as defiantly right-handed as Judaism and Christianity. According to one religious authority Allah has nothing left-handed about him at all, being the proud owner of two right hands, and in the Koran the chosen elect are placed on the Lord's right hand while the damned are condemned to his left side. When a pilgrim arrives at the Great Mosque in Mecca to fulfil one of the principal vows of his faith, he must enter with the right foot. In connection with Mecca, Muhammad is reputed to have said that the famous Black Stone sent by God as a cornerstone for his sacred dwelling is the '[right] hand of Allah upon the earth.' This was incorporated into the Kaaba, the most sacred shrine in Mecca, in the eastern and most propitious corner.

Some Islamic scholars caution the faithful to leave the mosque by the right foot, and interestingly add that they should leave the house to pay a call of nature by the left foot. In the world of Islam, above all others, the left hand and everything associated with it is unclean.

One English visitor to Egypt in the middle of the last century. E. W. Lane, gave a definitive account of the rituals observed by all Moslems at meal times, when all food is consumed from the right hand and nothing else; no cutlery and definitely no left hand, unless the right hand is either missing or totally paralysed.

After describing how the diners take up their positions round a tray on which the food is placed, sitting with their left knees on the floor and their right knees raised, he explains that they roll up their right sleeves to the elbow and tuck in to the meal using only the thumb and two fingers of the right hand to touch the food and convey it to their mouths. Lane then continues:

> It is a rule with the Muslims to honour the right hand above the left: to use the right hand for all honorable purposes, and the left for actions which, though necessary, are unclean . . .

He is of course referring to the common Middle Eastern custom of substituting the left hand and water for European lavatory paper, which makes it the Unclean Hand *par excellence*. He continues:

> At the ceremonial washing of hands, the Muslim faces the Koran. First the right hand is washed, then the left. The speaker says: 'Place the book of my actions in my right hand. Place not, as at the resurrection, the book of my actions in my left hand.'

Similar restrictions applied in many primitive societies. The French scholar Robert Hertz, who wrote one of the seminal essays on handedness and religion before he was tragically killed in the Great War, noted the widespread primitive custom applied to eating during mourning, in which neither hand was used. During this period the bereaved were either fed by others or ate their food with their mouths alone, like animals. As Hertz suggests, both hands were effectively paralysed in this case, though in normal circumstances the 'paralysis' only applied to the left hand. He quotes the custom among the tribes of lower Niger, where women were forbidden to use their left hands while cooking because of the accusation that those who did were practising sorcery or were trying to poison the food.

Hertz saw the relationship of left and right in terms of a fundamental polarity in which man saw himself and the world about him. Light was balanced by dark, heat with cold, good with evil, male with female, life with death, and in his own person right with left. At the root of all social and emotional characteristics Hertz saw an essential religious polarity that classified everything as either sacred or profane.

He asks in Ronald Needham's translation of his work *The Pre-Eminence of the Right Hand:*

> How could man's body, the microcosm, escape the law of polarity which governs everything? Society and the whole universe have a side which is sacred, noble, and precious, and another which is profane and common; a male side, strong and active, and another, female, weak and passive; or in two words, a right side and a left side . . .

A practical application of this belief in a religious setting was quoted by Hertz who commented that Hindus and Celts followed a specific ritual when endowing a person or object with good luck. The participants walked round the subject of their blessing three times from left to right, following the direction of the sun. The right sides of their bodies were turned inwards and from these the sacred and holy virtues they embodied radiated to the recipient. Walking in the opposite direction with the left side turned inwards was sacrilegious and unlucky.

From Buddhist prayer wheels which always rotate from left to right to the faith of ancient Egypt in which the eye of Hor, the god of the rising sun, was carried as an amulet and strongly associated with the right eye, the right hand has dominated most religions, in particular Christianity, where we started. In few places in the scriptures is the omnipotence of the right hand better described than in the opening to St Paul's epistle to the Hebrews, which reads:

> God, who at sundry times and in divers manners spake in time past unto the fathers by the prophets,

Hath in these last days spoken unto us by his Son, whom he hath appointed heir of all things, by whom also he made the worlds;

Who being the brightness of his glory, and express image of his person, and upholding all things by the word of his power, when he had by himself purged our sins, sat down on the right hand of the Majesty on high.

CHAPTER 4

The Devil's Hand

Habit, custom and religion have contributed in large measures to the almost institutionalized damnation and debasement of the left hand. Time-honoured stigmas have brought with them a huge cloud of superstition enveloping nearly every culture on earth in one form or another.

In its most extreme forms this superstition led to appalling acts of cruelty. An account of the practices of certain African tribes written in 1906 speaks of the people, presumably all right-handers, pouring boiling water into a hole in the ground, into which they thrust the left hand of any child who was showing signs of being naturally left-handed. The earth was rammed down around the tiny hand to ensure that it was scalded so effectively that the child would inevitably be forced to use its right hand. A similar account, this time of self-mutilation, was given by Evans-Pritchard in his study of *Nuer Spear Symbolism*. He records how young men in the tribe deliberately immobilized their left arms for months or even years by pressing metal rings deep into the flesh from the wrist upwards. These were forced in so tightly that they caused terrible pain and resulted in huge sores that effectively paralysed the offending limb.

As the weaker and non-aggressive hand the left was frequently associated with death and decay. North American Indians would cut off hands and fingers as sacrifices as well as punishments, and as with present-day insurance companies the loss of fingers from the left hand was thought less harmful than those from the right. From India itself comes an interesting version of the tale of Achilles' heel, in which the king's weak spot is his left hand.

In *The Story of the Human Hand*, Walter Sorell discusses the primitive male/female associations of right and left. He argues that in early agricultural societies in which women played a more prominent rôle 'the left side – the one to be protected – became the preferred side, but later, with man's growing supremacy, the left remained identified with the female and all female attributes.' In Sorell's opinion primitive man associated the left with danger, misfortune and weakness that had to be overcome in order to survive. In such societies the weak and old were frequently killed, so it was only natural that a symbolic 'killing' of everything associated with the left should take place. He concludes:

. . . the left hand has remained related to the life-giving, earth-bound, past-tied, motherly and creative concepts in contrast to the right hand, the male, the free, the active and aggressive . . .

This theme is explored also by Robert Hertz, who used the Maori culture as the source for much of his evidence on handedness. On the subject of gender classification he quotes the Maori 'tama tane' – the male side which is associated with: male virility, descent in the paternal line, the east and the creative force in the universe, as opposed to the 'tama mahine' – the female side which covered everything that was contrary. Among the Maori this seat of good and creative powers was on the right, or sacred side; the left was the profane side. The same held true in their religion, according to Hertz, with the gods sitting on the right and the demons on the left.

Very similar beliefs held sway in many parts of Africa too. In Bantu-speaking areas of the continent the right hand is often referred to as the *strong* or *male* hand; the left is less frequently known as the *inferior* or *female* hand. In West Africa the right hand is also called the 'eating hand', reinforcing the belief in the left as the Unclean Hand. Among the Ija tribe there used to be a rule that a woman should never touch her husband's face with her left hand; nor was she allowed to use it when cooking. The one notable concession to the left hand among the tribes of the area was the privilege accorded to Ibo warriors who had killed men with their own hands. They were allowed to drink with their left hands, perhaps as a gesture of having faced death and overcome it.

No, no, the <u>right</u> fist, O beloved!

Language has been one of the most significant ways through which prejudice against the left has been perpetuated and reinforced. Hertz has something to say about this too. He notes that in many languages there exists one word for *right* which is in constant use and a whole variety of euphemisms and slang words for *left*. Could this be an attempt to diminish the intrinsic evil in the left side by constantly obliterating its name, he asks, since the evil itself can never be totally abolished? He also considers the origin of the words for 'left' and 'right'. Picking on what he sees as a general assumption that *right* first meant the better hand and then by analogy the qualities of strength, virtue and skill that it came to manifest, he dismisses this argument by delving back into the origins of the Indo-European languages. Both the French word *droit* and the Armenian *adj*, he explains, expressed ideas of a force which went unerringly to its object following a regular and constant path, as opposed to a tortuous and oblique route, and had this meaning before they were applied to one side of the body.

Two of the commonest words in English with specific 'left' and 'right' connotations and origins are *sinister* and *dextrous*, which both came from Latin words. *Sinister* is a Latin adjective meaning 'on the left hand/side', with its own root in the noun for a 'pocket' *sinus*. (Roman togas were made with the pocket on the left.) It also had two contradictory meanings used in connection with prediction or augury. One of these amounted to our understanding of the English word *sinister*, but the other meant 'auspicious, lucky'. The reason for these diametrically opposed interpretations is linked with the favoured side of augury, which is dealt with later. In brief the Romans at first regarded the *left* as the fortunate side, but later adopted the Greek method of taking the auspices, which placed the right in this favoured position. As you might imagine, the Greeks have a lot to answer for among sinistrals!

Because the Greeks regarded the left as inauspicious and unlucky their word for 'left', *skaios*, came to mean 'ill-omened' and 'awkward' as well. This in turn influenced another Latin word for 'left', the adjective *scaevus*, which inherited similar meanings. And from *scaevus* came the epithet *Scaevola* which was given to the Mucius clan after one of their number, Caius Macius, sneaked into Lars Porsenna's camp with the aim of killing him, and when discovered before carrying out his mission burned off his own right hand. Left and good fortune seldom went hand in hand in the ancient world.

The Latin adjective *dexter*, meaning 'on the right side', had a far more favourable genealogy and legacy. Thanks to Greek divination again, it developed from the Greek word *dexios*, meaning 'right-handed' and by association 'clever' and 'skilful'. Our English word 'dextrous' is blessed with the same meanings and according to the *Oxford Dictionary of English Etymology*: 'The primary meaning passes sometimes into "south", sometimes into "adroit" and "valiant".'

'Adroit' has obvious associations with the French *à droit*, 'to the right' (and all other qualities associated with *droit*). 'Valiant' is linked by the same original belief. But 'south' is interesting and broadens the investigation into languages of other regions, notably Arabic, which derives from a different source to the Indo-European group.

The primitive division of the universe into two opposing elements and the corresponding division of the human frame that mirrored these led in many languages to the same words denoting the sides of the body and the points of the compass. Hertz, who makes this point, quotes the Irish word *dess*, which means 'right' and 'south'.

The Arabic word *yamīn* is derived from the verb *yamana* which means 'to be lucky, fortunate' and has as a secondary meaning 'to go to the right'. *Yamīn* itself also has meanings associated with oath-taking (with the right hand of course), which explains its principal modern meaning 'right side: right hand'. The geographical significance is found in another word that comes from the same verb *al-yaman*, the Arabic name for the Yemen. Now the Yemen was the *Arabia Felix* of the ancient world, the fruitful land of good luck, good fortune, prosperity and success, all of which are neatly summed up in another Arabic word from the same root, *yumn*. The Yemen was also the land of the south, which lay on the right side of any Arab who turned to the east to see the rising sun, pray and make his prophecies.

On the other side in every respect lay the land of the north, the left side and misfortune. In its geographical location this is Syria, or in its Arabic name *aš-ša'm*, which is related to *šu'm*, 'bad luck, calamity, evil omen and misfortune'. Another word for the north is *šamāl* or *šimāl* which also means 'left side; left'. So the polarities on both sides lie deeply rooted in the language.

The same is true in another Semitic language, Hebrew, in which the Benjamites (whom we have already met), or Yaminites, as they are so called, were the sons of the right as well as the sons of the south, while the Sim'alites were both the sons of the north and left. (The paradox here of course is that in the Bible the *Benjamites* appear to be singled out for their left-handedness!)

The nearest we can get in English to this symmetry between hand and compass is in the term *southpaw*, an American word today applied to boxers who lead with their right hands while guarding with the left. It originated not in the ring, in fact, but in the diamond – the baseball diamond of Chicago's West Side stadium. In 1890 this was sited to protect batters from the late afternoon sun. As a result the pitcher faced west and if he was left-handed his pitching hand was on the south side, making him a southpaw.

The Japanese word for 'left', *hidari*, originates from the words for *sun* and *on*, which reflect the custom followed by the Emperors of facing south on ceremonial occasions, so that the sun rose on the left or propitious side.

Other words for 'left' or its derivatives show by now predictable etymologies. The Italian *mancini* can also mean 'crooked' and even 'maimed'. In Spanish the word for 'left', *zurdo*, gives rise to the phrase *no ser zurdo*, meaning 'to be clever', in other words 'not to be left-handed'; and the phrase *a zurdas* means 'the wrong way'. *Gauche*, which found its way into English in the middle of the 18th century when the *Oxford English Dictionary* first notes its use at the hands of Lord Chesterfield, seems to have come from the verb *gauchir*, 'to warp, turn aside', from which its present meanings of awkward and clumsy derive. In German *links* means 'left' and the adjective *linkisch* means 'awkward'. From here it is only a short step to our own word.

Seeking the origins of 'right' and 'left', Martin Gardiner voices a popular idea in his book *The Ambidextrous Universe*, namely that:

> Our word 'right' suggests that it is right to use the right hand. It may be that 'left' had its origin in the fact that the left hand is so little used that it is 'left out' of most tasks.

This is an engaging idea but one that smacks of being a touch too simple in the face of the evidence provided by the *Oxford English Dictionary*, which after noting the Old

English spelling *left* (originally from Kent) and the Middle English variant *lift*, adds the glossary:

> the primary sense 'weak, worthless' is represented also in East Fris. [Frisian] *luf*, Du. [Dutch] dial. *loof*, and the derived sense 'left' (hand) in M. Du. [Middle Dutch], L.G. [Low German] *luchter, lucht, luft,* North Fris. *leeft, leefter.*
> Cf. further (though connexion is very doubtful) O.E. [Old English] *léf* weak, *léfung* paralysis . . .

As for *left-handed* the OED lists several meanings, two of which it acknowledges as obsolete:

1. Having the left hand more serviceable than the right; using the left hand by preference . . .
2. a. Crippled, defective *Obs.* b. Awkward; clumsy, inapt c. Characterized by underhand dealings *Obs.* . . .
3. Ambiguous, doubtful, questionable. In medical language: Spurious . . .
4. Ill-omened, inauspicious, sinister. Of a deity: Unpropitious . . .
5. Of a marriage: *Literally*, one in which the bridegroom gives the bride his left hand instead of the right . . . [this is the morganatic marriage mentioned earlier]
6. In various uses. a. Of an implement: adapted to the l. hand or arm, for use by a left-handed person. b. Placed on the left hand. c. Of a blow: Delivered by the left hand . . .
7. In scientific and technical use: Characterized by a direction of rotation to the left; producing such a rotation in the plane of a polarized ray . . .

As a passing shot the great dictionary includes the word *left-handiness* which it defines as an 'awkward manner' and illustrates with another quotation from the inestimable Lord Chesterfield dated 1749:

> An awkward address, ungraceful attitudes and actions, and a certain left-handiness (if I may use that word) loudly proclaim low education.

There are millions of sinistrals who would happily come to blows with him to show why he may not use 'that word', but there's no denying that the prejudice against the left hand is as firmly rooted in English as it is in many other languages. English also serves as a valid example of Robert Hertz's point made earlier that many languages contain a great variety of euphemisms for the left and left-handedness. Probably the most commonly used is *cack-handed*, which comes from the word *cack*, meaning excrement. So here we immediately find a reference to the Unclean Hand which has cropped up in many other parts of the world. *Cack-handed* has many derivatives, as have lots of other words, though from their bizarre appearance it would be difficult to recognize them. The list below presents a selection to prove Hertz's point. (They all mean the same thing – 'left-handed'!)

Back-handed	(South)
Ballock-handed	(Bristol)
Bang-handed	(TyneTees)
Bawky-handed	(North)
Ca-pawed	(Lancashire)
Cam-handed	(South)
Cat-handed	(Devon)
Cledhec	(Cornwall)
Clicky-handed	(Cornwall)
Coochy-handed	(South)
Cork-handed	(Derbyshire)
Corrie-pawed	(Scotland)
Cow-pawed	(North)
Cowie-handed	(North)
Cowley-handed	(North)
Cuddy-handed	(Durham)
Cuddy-wifter	(North)

Dawky-handed	(Yorkshire)
Dollock-handed	(North)
Dolly-pawed	(Yorkshire)
Gallock-handed	(Yorkshire)
Gammy-handed	(South)
Gar-pawed	(North)
Gawky-handed	(Scotland)
Gawp-handed	(North)
Golly-handed	(North)
Kack-handed	(North)
Kay-fisted	(Lancashire)
Kay-pawed	(North)
Ketty-handed	(Somerset)

Keggy-handed	(West Midlands)
Keir-pawed	(Scotland)
Kittagh-handed	(North)
Marlborough-handed	(South)
Scoochy-handed	(South)
Scrammy-handed	(Bristol)
Scroochy-handed	(South)
Skiffle-handed	(South)
Skiffy-handed	(South)
Skivvy-handed	(South)
Spuddy-handed	(Gloucestershire)
Squiffy-handed	(South)
Squippy-handed	(Wiltshire)
Wacky-handed	(Midlands)
Watty-handed	(South)

As for one of the commonest uses of the word *left* today, its political application, this seems to have come into use in France during the *ancien régime* before the French Revolution, when the nobles took their seats on the right side of the King in the National Assembly and the capitalists on his left. This was taken to imply that the right was equated with the prevalent social order and the left with shady, subversive elements seeking to usurp the traditional *status quo*.

So ingrained has this attitude towards the left become throughout civilization that Robert Hertz was able to draw anthropological evidence to show that many primitive peoples, in particular the Indians of North America, didn't even need words to convey the 'sinister' role of the left hand. They developed a simple sign language using only movements of their heads and arms which allowed them to communicate quite effectively.

In this basic vocabulary of gestures the right hand

represented *me*; the left hand *not-me*, in other words everyone else. *High* could be shown by raising the right hand above the left, which was held flat and motionless like the horizon. *Low* was represented by the reverse action, holding the left hand below the right. And a raised right hand implied all the masculine attributes of virility, bravery and power, though the same hand moved to the left side could mean, according to the context, destruction, death or burial.

Judged in this light it is easy to see how prejudice and superstition became almost automatic, and when the element of luck was added to the equation, anything vaguely sinister scarcely had a look in. Even medical science succumbed. The Greek physician, Galen, believed that the womb was divided into two parts which produced boys from (you've guessed it) the right side and girls from the left. Others held a modified view that girls came from the left testicle, boys from the right.

Many Romans employed slaves for the sole purpose of standing at the entrance of their houses to make sure that every guest entered the master's house with his or her right foot first. Some believe they were the origin of the word 'footman'.

One notable group to contravene this practice are Freemasons, who from early times appear to have followed the military tradition of leading with the left foot, the one which gives the best balance when setting off with a heavy weapon on the left of one's body. Freemasons were allowed to step with the left foot onto the threshold of their lodge, provided the next step across the threshold and into the lodge was made with the right foot.

Freemasonry has taken quite an interest in the left hand. The ritual punishment for divulging secrets is to have the right hand cut off and slung over the left shoulder on the end of a cord, 'there to wither and die'. And apprentices who present themselves for initiation must appear with their left trouser leg torn open at the knee, symbolizing the fact that, like the left knee, the apprentice is the weakest part of the Masonic body.

In popular folklore the devil has always been left-handed. How could the Prince of Darkness be anything else? Whether holding out his hand to greet a newly won convert or brandishing a sword against goodness and righteousness, it is always his left hand which is dominant. In a similar way, moving from right to left, anti-clockwise, has always been seen as moving in the devil's direction, contrary to the hallowed movement of divine power as manifested in the sun. The examples of moving 'sunways', or circumambulation as it is known, are legion. In 1900 J. G. Campbell wrote a book called *Superstitions of Scotland*, which catalogued some typical examples of the importance attached to *deiseal*, the Gaelic word for moving to the right:

> The rule is *deiseal* for everything. This is the manner in which screw nails are driven, and is common with many for no reason but its convenience. Old men in the Highlands were very particular about it. The coffin was taken *deiseal* about the grave, when about to be lowered . . . When putting a straw rope on a house or corn-stack, if the assistant went *tuaitheal* [against the sun] the old man was ready to come down and thrash him. On coming to a house, the visitor should go round it *deiseal* to secure luck on the object of his visit. The word is from *deas*, right-hand, and *iul*, direction, and of itself makes no reference to the sun.

There are countless examples of circumambulation from all over the world. Hindu brides lead their husbands three times round the sacred fire at the marriage ceremony. Fathers in the Baltic state of Estonia were once obliged to run round the church at their children's baptism. In the *Iliad* Homer describes how Achilles made three circuits of the funeral pyre of his friend Patroclus. And the Buddhist Wheel of Life is for ever revolving from left to right.

Moving widdershins, or in the opposite direction to the sun, was a cast-iron way of calling up the devil or any evil spirit you care to mention. The whole cult of the Black Mass revolved around a deliberate inversion of the Christian liturgy, with the left hand taking pride of place in performing symbolic rites and holy scriptures recited backwards to pander to the demons being worshipped. In northern England there was a popular tradition that a man who ran three times widdershins round a church at night would see the devil looking at him from under the porch. If you move widdershins round a room three times in the dark and then look in a mirror you're sure to see the devil in the glass. The Church too follows this course in exorcism where the ceremonial circuit is made in the wrong direction, i.e. widdershins, presumably to call up the offending spirit and banish it all the more easily.

Even on a social level, such an inversion can have devastating results. Passing or pouring the wine at table with the left hand is a sure sign of bad luck and passing the wine anti-clockwise was as good as black-balling oneself from respectable society. Calling for a Left-handed Toast was tantamount to putting a curse on the victim. Two Wiltshire families, the Hartgills and the Stourtons, enjoyed a lengthy feud in the middle of the sixteenth century in which such a toast featured from the outset. According to the *Wiltshire Archeological Magazine* of July 1864, Lord Stourton was wining and dining with a group of his chums and retainers at Stourton Hall a few days after he and William Hartgill had 'falled utterly out'. Towards the end of the meal his lordship got to his feet and, holding up his glass, announced: 'Gentlemen, the toast is the Hartgill family – left-handed.' The company took up his cry to a man and downed their wine with relish. It took seventeen years to sort out the matter and get the two families back on speaking terms!

In Tibet there is a saying: 'Beware the devils on the left-hand side', and it is these devils which have to be placated whenever we spill salt (as Judas Iscariot apparently did at the Last Supper). Salt of course was more than a condiment in the ancient world. It was almost the stuff of life itself, and from the Latin name for it, *sal*, and its derivative *salarium* (the money given to Roman soldiers to buy salt), we get the word 'salary'.

It was the Roman writer Plutarch who first drew our attention to the hazardous business of sneezing. Apparently a sneeze to the right presages good luck; one to the left is more than a little careless.

Even involuntary itchings and twitchings are imbued with their own ominous significance. A twitching right eye indicates that you are going to see a friend. If it is the left eye that tips you the wink, watch out for an enemy. In Morocco a twitch in the left eye carries even greater foreboding, warning of a death in the family or some equal catastrophe.

In Scotland an itching right palm brings the happy news that it will soon receive money. When the left palm itches the money will be going, not coming. (In Germany the reverse is true!)

In parts of Africa the twitching of your right sole announces the arrival of a man. When the left sole twitches a woman is on her way to see you. Feet also play an important part in controlling man's fate, as exemplified by the Roman slaves who safeguarded domestic good fortune by preventing anyone from entering the house with the left foot first. The superstitions connected with feet go far beyond this however. Among the Loango people of Africa it is considered essential to leave either one's bed or the hut with the right foot first. Had they met Dr Johnson, he would have agreed whole-heartedly. He never gave precedence to the left foot in important matters like entering a house since he believed 'to enter the house with skir or left foot foremost brings down evil on the inmates.'

Mixing up your shoes and feet can lead to terrible trouble too. According to Pliny, the otherwise canny emperor Augustus Caesar nearly came horribly unstuck when he 'put his left shoe for his right' and barely escaped with his life when his troops came in search of a pay rise.

The appearance of birds on one side or the other is traditionally linked with augury and has been regarded as one of the primary omens since earliest times. In many cultures specific birds bring their own indications of what the future holds in store. Among the Masai again, a man on his way to visit a sick woman will know that she is gravely ill if the ol-tilo bird sings on the left-hand side of his path. But if he hears the bird singing on the right his step can quicken in the happy knowledge that the patient is on the mend.

In the British Isles the magpie is one of the principal birds of omen, and in Ireland in particular seeing three magpies on the left while you are travelling is a bad sign, but a pair spotted on your right indicate that all will be well.

The left hand has a part to play in affairs of the heart as well. One rather extreme Irish remedy for anyone having trouble in getting their message across was to write a letter 'of most desperate love with a raven's quill in the blood of the ring finger of the left hand'.

According to Robert Hertz, the Maoris have a different way of winning hearts. To start with the lover needs to be afloat in his canoe where he can judge the direction of the wind. If it is blowing in his true love's direction 'he takes a feather in his left hand, passes it under his left thigh, and then holding it upright in his out-thrust left hand, he recites his charm, which concludes with an appeal to the winds to waft hitherward the desired woman'. For once it's reassuring to find the left hand having some positive value!

After this dismal category of superstition stacked so unremittingly against the left hand, it's only fair to end with an effort to try and redress the balance. Left-handers rejoice! Not *all* the actions and associations of your dominant hand herald disaster and calamity. In one or two instances they can actually be beneficial. There was an Inca chief who clearly thought this was the case. His name was Lloque Yupanqui, which actually means 'left-handed'. Some Masai also ask for long life and strength with their left hands. They do this at the time of the new moon by throwing a stone or branch at the moon as they make their wish.

In another part of Africa, this time Ghana (still the Gold Coast when this event took place), a major-general in the British army went to greet a local chief recently defeated in the Ashanti wars and held out his right hand as a gesture of conciliation. Seeing this, the chief told him that it was his native custom to greet the bravest warriors with the left hand and they shook in this way. The major-general's name was Baden-Powell and the handshake was later adopted for the Boy Scout movement that he founded.

A much earlier legend recalls a similar event in the career of Alexander the Great, who in his wanderings around the Middle East and Central Asia, apparently came across an entirely left-handed tribe who regarded shaking hands with the left hand as a supreme distinction since the left hand was the one nearer the heart.

Apart from these isolated cases the only culture which does not appear to have an unequivocal dextral outlook is that of China. Here there has never been a tradition of absolute polarity governing every facet of life from getting out of bed in the morning to paying respect to the gods. In China each case is judged in its own right and is given a dominant polarity according to what appears to be most fitting. As in most aspects of Chinese life the rules of handedness are far from simple. Greetings, for example, differ according to sex. A boy traditionally covered his right hand with his left when he was taught to bow. His sister was given the opposite instruction and had to conceal her left hand and present her right.

Those about to be punished in China had to bare their right shoulders. Left shoulders were bared when you were on your way to a party or any other fun and games.

Chinese doctors used to predict the sex of infants before birth by feeling where the embryo lay in the mother. If it lay on the right that baby was reckoned to be a girl; if on the left a boy. This introduces the underlying principle of handedness and virtually everything else in China – the doctrine of Yin and Yang. These were the two forces that divided the universe. Yang belonged to the male and was connected with all things left. Yin belonged to the female and governed everything on the right.

Now this seems to be at odds with the principles and superstitions that existed almost everywhere else on earth, but the Chinese have never shown much concern, or respect, for global uniformity. One ingenious explanation put forward for their system, certainly as it affects etiquette, is that the *chief* travelled as a passenger in his chariot with two of his bodyguard. One of these was the driver who naturally rode in the middle to control the team of horses. The second man was a spearman whose job it was to protect his master and who consequently stood on the right to make the best use of his fighting arm (even in China right-handers predominate). Therefore the only place for the chief to travel was on the left side of the carriage. Thus, the reasoning follows, the left became the place of honour.

That said, Chinese etiquette is governed by the need to reflect the dominance of Yin or Yang in every particular circumstance. In one situation it may be ruled that the forces of Yin are dominant, in which case the right will take precedence; in another, when Yang is supreme, the left leads. As a result, Chinese superstition and lore is largely free of the over-bearing prejudices and fears that surround left-handedness in most other parts of the world.

CHAPTER 5

Fatal Attractions

Our curiosity to peer into the future and discover what lies in store has always been insatiable. Today we may reckon that we are hard-headed and logical in our approach to forecasting, calling on vast banks of data to predict economic trends and political developments with the same scientific assurance as the man on the television telling us about tomorrow's weather. Yet this doesn't prevent a good many newspapers and magazines from printing regular horoscopes; nor does it stop professional fortune tellers from making a tidy living from filling in a few personal details for those clients keen to narrow down the predictions aimed at several million of their fellow countrymen on the breakfast television show.

Luck and the left hand extends quite naturally into the more serious business of divining what's going to happen to each of us in the weeks or years ahead.

At the simplest level come predictions based on the human body. If you feel the bumps on someone's head and apply the guidelines laid down by students of phrenology you'll apparently be able to tell a good deal about their lives past and future. At least that's what many Victorians felt when phrenology was making a big splash as a parlour entertainment. (Palm reading, to give the study its popular name, features later, and is the most comprehensive form of 'body' fortune telling).

Even innocent moles can be steeped in meaning for those who have eyes to see, and the ones with specific left-sided significance show a predominance of unfortunate or undesirable traits. So the next time you're giving yourself the once over in the mirror before getting dressed, see what your body can tell you about yourself (apart from the need to show less enthusiasm for riding in lifts and habitually having a couple of Scotches at lunch).

Working from your feet upwards, moles on the following parts of your body reveal:

Left foot	– Quick thinking and intelligence
Ankle (either)	– Tendency to foppishness (in men); hard work and drive (in women)
Leg (either)	– Laziness
Left knee	Impetuosity
Left thigh	– Isolation, poverty, loss – nice warm temperament, though
Hips (either)	– Healthy and plentiful offspring
Left ribs	– Tendency to be idle, insensitive, cowardly and discourteous – in spite of this, humorous
Back (anywhere)	– Open, generous, showy and arrogant. Low down moles show sensuousness and self-indulgence!
Abdomen (anywhere)	– Selfishness, greed, laziness
Left breast	– Strong-willed, sometimes leading to ill-judged attachments (in women); wealth and happiness (in men)
Shoulder (either)	– Tough times
Left arm	– Money worries
Hand (either)	– Success
Left cheek	– Problems and struggles
Ear (either)	– Recklessness
Left eyebrow	– Problem marriage

| *Eye (either)* | – (Near outer corner) thrift, frugality and calm |
| *Left forehead* | – Extravagance and feebleness |

Not that all fortune telling necessarily sets out to provide specific answers and information about the future. Many methods, including some of the oldest, only offer a 'Yes' or 'No' to questions already asked. There's a popular tradition that you can get a positive or negative answer in this way by using a gold wedding ring. This has to be tied to a length of black thread and then lowered into a glass of water with the left hand. If the ring touches the left side of the glass the answer to the question is 'No'; if it touches the right side it's 'Yes'; and if it touches either the side nearest or furthest from you the fates need a bit longer to make up their mind and shouldn't be consulted for another 24 hours.

Animals and birds have always played an important part in fortune telling, preferably in a recently sacrificed state when their entrails could be inspected by the officiating experts to see what was going to happen. Whole treatises were written on ways of divining by studying the liver alone. In the case of birds, their unpredictable but very positive flight has always inspired fortune tellers to look on them as messengers of the gods, bringing divine approval or censure for vital decisions about to be taken. This rule applies to most flights of birds, but there are those special cases, whether in the air or sitting in a tree, that have always carried a portent of their own. Crows seen on the left have never been a good omen. Hawks on the left warn of enemies. A magpie seen on the left warns of death. The only bird it's safe to see on the left is the wagtail, it seems, since this invariably brings good luck in its wake.

The name given to this type of divination is *augury*, a practice which was refined with great care in the ancient world. It seems to have developed in Italy, where the Etruscans developed a number of Eastern rites into a complicated code that required a select body of augurs to implement and observe. The Romans took over these earlier traditions and refined them still further into a well-institutionalized body which wielded growing power and influence. Many of the greatest Romans – Caesar, Pompey, Pliny, Antony and Cicero – were augurs, one of a body of sixteen whose job it was to interpret signs sent from the gods and act accordingly.

Cicero also wrote one of the most detailed accounts of augury and that we owe much of our knowledge on the subject is due to him, especially its bearing on handedness, which played such an important part in the later dominance of the right hand.

When the Romans started in the augury business, the augurs faced south as they watched for the signs from the gods. In this position the left was considered the lucky side. Then everything was turned round the other way when Rome conquered Greece and adopted the Greek system in which the augurs faced north, putting the east with its rising sun on the right, so making the right hand the favoured one. It's because of this simple turn-around that there has been so much left-handed suffering (in Europe at least) ever since!

The Roman augury that developed from this change had a clearly defined ritual. Auspices were studied on any important matter: elections to important public offices, declaring war, laying the foundations for sacred buildings and temples, or marriage. Before seeking the gods' veto or approval of the proposition to be put forward, the augur would mark out a rectangle with his curved stick of office and then, standing in the centre of this, he traced a similar rectangle in the sky indicating the area in which auspices had to appear. Then the question was put to the gods and a magistrate scanned the skies to see where the birds appeared. Once seen these were studied by the augur who interpreted the gods' answer from their movements. As a result, the augurs had an effective veto on all state policy. Omens could be nullified if they were flawed in some way. They could even be nullified some time later if the augur deemed that all had not in fact been as it should with the omen. Cicero had good reason for calling the augurs 'the highest and most responsible authorities in the state', and once consecrated an augur held his post for life.

Probably the most important omen ever seen over Rome was that which decided the city's name and chose its founder. Romulus and Remus grew into rivals over the foundation of the city and, as Cicero describes, decided the matter by observing bird flight at dawn:

> Then Remus took the auspices alone
> And waited for the lucky bird; while on
> The lofty Aventine fair Romulus
> His quest did keep to wait the soaring tribe:
> Their contest would decide the city's name
> As Rome, or Remora . . .

The other augurs stood on the Capitoline hill from where, at dawn, they saw a bird flying to the left, indicating that the gods had chosen Romulus to found the city. (In those days the left was the lucky side.) This was still the case in 86 B.C. when Gaius Marius waited in exile for a sign that would herald his return to Rome, where he had been elected consul no fewer than seven times. He kept his eyes peeled for an eagle and, as Cicero tells us:

When Marius, reader of divine decrees,
Observed the bird's auspicious, gliding course,
He recognized the goodly sign foretold,
That he in glory would return to Rome;
Then on the left, Jove's thunder pealed aloud
And thus declared the eagle omen true.

Thunder and lightning, again unpredictable phenomena, were as important omens as birds' flight and song, and here again the side on which they appeared was the deciding factor. This helps to explain why the Latin word *sinister* can mean both 'auspicious, lucky' and 'inauspicious, unlucky'. In the days when Roman augurs faced south to study their auspices the left, *sinister*, side was the favoured one. The opposite meaning only came into force when the augurs made a U-turn and faced north.

In those good old days when the left hand was still favourite, it had its part to play in healing too. Writing in his *Natural History*, Pliny included a number of cures that incorporated it. Sufferers from earache could cure the condition with a spider that had been caught in the left hand and then boiled in oil. The left eye of a frog came in handy for inflamed eyes. The frog's eye was applied to the patient's own left eye and the inflammation was sure to recede. If scrofula was your trouble, Pliny recommended a dead man's hand, an interesting idea bearing in mind that in more recent times sufferers of scrofula were said to be cured by the royal touch. Dr Johnson had scrofula as a child and was reputedly one of the last to be touched like this. Presumably by that time the penny had dropped that, no doubt like the frog cure, this was so much eyewash.

Other ancient cures included one for hiccups which involved slipping a ring over the ring finger of the left hand. Another involved applying a hot dried bean to the right elbow to relieve toothache in the left jaw. And a striking remedy for gippy tummy called for the victim to stick his left thumb into the offending part of his belly while reciting 'Adam bedam alam betoir alun botum'.

The Age of Enlightment didn't entirely neglect this branch of medicine either. In 1731 the author of *The Poor Man's Physician* suggested this as a possible way to stop bleeding:

> Take a toad and dry it very well before the sun, then put it in a linen cloth, and hang it with string over the part which bleedeth, and hang it so low that it may touch the breast on the left side, near the heart. This will stay all bleeding at the mouth, nose, wound, or anything whatsoever.

In many people's eyes the left hand itself has an even more important application when it comes under the scrutiny of a real Romany fortune teller. There's always been a debate between palmists about the different values to give to the readings of each hand, but the Romanies have traditionally never been in any doubt. For them the whole story is hidden in the left hand. The right hand occasionally gets a glance, but this is incidental to the principal study of the 'mounts', 'markings' and 'lines' seen on the left palm and the very shape of the hand itself.

Palmistry is divided into two distinct studies – chirognomy, which is concerned with analysing the shape of the hand to determine a subject's psychological and emotional make-up, and chiromancy, which concentrates on the lines in the palm to peer into the future and foretell what lies waiting there to be discovered and experienced.

Modern sceptics dismiss a lot of the Romany lore and seek to replace it with scientifically verifiable techniques of palm reading. However, most experts acknowledge that there is some bizarre connection between the shape and markings on our hands and our lives, both past and future. Others are less easily impressed by modern dismissals and cling to Romany lore which is well rooted in history. India and Egypt seem likely sites for the origin of the study. The Chinese got in on the act as early as five thousand years ago. The Greeks dabbled in it too, with Aristotle going as far as calling the hand 'the organ of organs', and Romanies have been wandering round the world peering at left hands and leaving a trail of hopes and anxieties behind them for longer than anyone knows. What do they look at? The answer is everything, but the study is carefully arranged to ensure that nothing is overlooked. Enter chirognomy.

One look at a hand can tell a trained Romany fortune teller a lot about your character. The shape of the hand and the length of the fingers are the main features. The shape of the thumb is very important and the texture of the skin has its part to play too.

The Spatulate Hand

As its name suggests, this hand has fingers shaped like spatulas, wider at the top than at the bottom. The palms tend to be large and broad too. It is a powerful, positive, active hand – one that speaks of self-confidence, drive and energy.

The Conic Hand

Hands with a tapering palm that is narrower at the finger tips than at the wrist are traditionally associated with a creative, impulsive temperament, which leads to its other popular name – the *artistic hand*. Small thumbs are another common feature and they too point to a personality that can be easily swayed by emotions or other powerful forces. Short-lived as these trends may be they are always pursued with vigour and total absorption.

The Square Hand

This is the steady, trustworthy, practical hand. It may lack the flair and initiative of other hands but it shows a reliable, constant dependability which is upright, honest and strong. A little unimaginative perhaps, but rock solid.

The Pointed Hand

Shortish fingers and a long palm hint at a quick-thinking, energetic and inspired personality. This is often a slightly intolerant one that prefers to go its own way rather than wait for slower ones to catch up. Intellectual, aesthetic and ascetic, this hand points to a spirit that values beauty but doesn't mind isolation to enjoy it.

The Mixed Hand

Hands that feature characteristics of some or all the other types naturally show a breadth of talents and characteristics. These are versatile and talented hands, but also ones that can show intolerance and a tendency to try and cover a wide field in preference to concentrating on one definite pursuit.

Other features about the hand in general can help fill in the picture. The size is important. Small hands denote intuitive, fast-acting, impulsive personalities, while large hands reflect a contemplative disposition, one that prefers to weigh up a situation before acting. In the same way hard, tough skin can suggest a 'thick-skinned' attitude; soft, yielding skin is more sensitive. Turning to the fingers, a quick study of the joints will tell if the subject has an eye for detail, neatness and concentration, which is indicated by knotty joints. Before studying the fingers individually the Romany will take note of the thumb, one of the most important guides in chirognomy. Sir Isaac Newton once commented that, in the absence of any other proofs, the thumb itself would convince him of God's existence. For the thumb is the paramount symbol of Man's distinction from the rest of the animal kingdom. In its separation from the other four fingers it allows man a mobility that far outreaches that of any other creature. Space, distance and dimension take on a new meaning, making the thumb almost the hallmark of *homo sapiens*. As the French writer Malcolm de Chazal remarked shrewdly, 'the fingers must be educated – the thumb is born knowing'.

A Romany will study the thumb in the light of the three dominant powers that govern the universe: will power, logic and love. As a general rule of (dare one say it) thumb, the longer the thumb the greater the subject's will power and the greater his or her impact on the world. A study of the great men of history has shown a high percentage with noticeably long thumbs.

The top, nail segment is related specifically to will. If it is large and broad it shows an abundance of determination and the ability to stick at anything. Narrow nail segments, particularly those that end in a point, suggest wasted effort.

Logic resides in the second segment which again is judged by its size and breadth. A good, thick segment represents control, well-tuned powers of reason, and consequently a tendency towards caution. A thinner, narrower segment points to the opposite tendencies, a lack of control and impulsiveness.

Now study the relative length of these two segments. Whichever is the longer will indicate the dominant polarity in your psyche, reason or will.

Love and powerful emotions are shown by a thumb that is fleshy and broad at the top. Similarly a wide angle between thumb and index finger when the hand is spread shows a generous disposition; a narrow one hints at closeness and excessive caution in dealings with others.

Now for the fingers, each of which is influenced by one of the astrological bodies. (As a general rule long fingers are indicative of a less active, more temperamental character; short fingers demonstrate action and energy.)

The Index Finger

This is the finger of Jupiter, sometimes called the 'finger of ambition'. It is usually read in conjunction with the thumb next door, and suggests the intensity and desires in life for which the thumb's energy is provided. A long index finger is a sign of ambition; a short one a sign of insecurity and a desire to keep out of the limelight.

The Second Finger

Also called the middle finger, this is under the influence of Saturn and gives a good indication of the subject's overall balance. A long second finger shows a reasoning temperament that may tend to over-intellectualize life's decisions. A short second finger indicates the opposite – an intuitive reaction to life in which the heart clearly governs the head.

Ring Finger

We have already seen the importance attached to this finger in a number of instances, and as the finger of Apollo it is strongly linked with the emotions. A ring finger that is out of balance with the rest of the hand suggests an emotional life that is either too active and energetic or one that is cramped, withdrawn and stifled.

Little Finger

This is Mercury's finger and like the index finger should be read in conjunction with the one next to it, in this case, the ring finger. Read together they give an idea of how well the subject gets on with other people. If the little finger is clearly separated from the rest it shows a detached personality that may have trouble establishing relationships. If the little finger is slightly twisted, it can also point to a twisted and untruthful nature.

Before leaving the fingers Romanies study the nails as markers of physical condition as well as of fate. Bluish nails suggest poor circulation and possibly heart trouble. Long, fluted nails are taken to be a sign of respiratory problems. Short, round nails are seen as a sign of throat complaints. And on the fate front, Romanies interpret white flecks in nails as follows:

> On the thumb as a sign of travel
> On the index finger as a sign of enmity
> On the second finger as a sign of future changes
> On the ring finger as a sign of anxieties
> On the little finger as a sign of good luck

The Mounts of the Left Hand

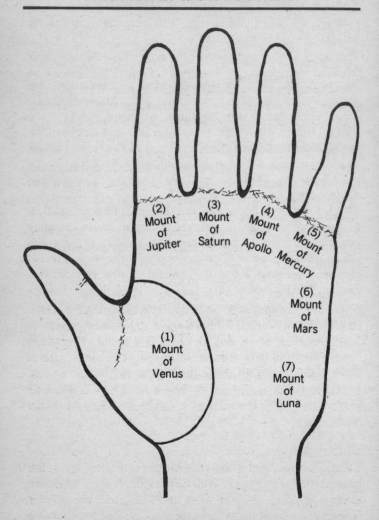

(2)
Mount
of
Jupiter

(3)
Mount
of
Saturn

(4)
Mount
of
Apollo

(5)
Mount
of
Mercury

(6)
Mount
of
Mars

(1)
Mount
of
Venus

(7)
Mount
of
Luna

After the fingers come the study of the palm itself, starting with the raised, fleshy areas known as the Mounts.

Mount of Venus

This is the large, fleshy pad at the base of the thumb and is the seat of energy. If it is well developed it shows an affectionate, sensuous make-up, with powerful physical needs. If the mount is small or non-existent, the opposite is true, showing a cold, unemotional frame of mind.

Mount of Luna

This is the mount of the Moon across the hand from the Mount of Venus. When normally developed this is a sign of an imaginative spirit, though if it is too prominent this imagination can spill over into fanaticism. Where there is no Mount of Luna there is also likely to be a marked absence of artistic appreciation and no awareness of beauty.

Mounts of Mars

These are the marks of courage. The mount lying above the Mount of Venus, referred to as the Lower Mount of Mars, implies when well developed a quiet, controlled courage in moments of extreme danger. The other, Upper Mount of Mars, lying above the Mount of Luna, is a mark of moral courage when well developed. If it is weak or absent altogether the subject is not the type destined for martyrdom.

Mount of Jupiter

Coming to the fingers now, the Mount of Jupiter lies at the base of the index finger. Well developed, it shows a desire to reap full rewards from work and home life, though if it is very prominent it can indicate a selfish and overbearing

nature. When underdeveloped, the Mount of Jupiter reflects a lack of drive and ambition.

Mount of Saturn

Of all the mounts this one below the second finger is likely to be the least developed, which is a good thing in fact. A plain, smooth mount is a sign of an untroubled life. The more apparent it is, the more serious a temperament it reflects, and when it is well developed Romanies take it as a sure sign of a depressive and brooding attitude to life.

Mount of Apollo

Coming below the ring finger this mount, when normally developed, is a sign of a cheerful attitude combined with an artistic and sensitive temperament. These can be taken to extremes if the mount is over-developed, leading to egocentricity and affectation. Where the mount is flat there is also likely to be an absence of aesthetic and cultural awareness.

Mount of Mercury

This little mount beneath the little finger is the home of wit, mental agility and intelligence. When over-developed this can lead to deceitfulness and dishonesty. When the mount is small and insignificant it's a sign of the exact opposite – a dull, tardy temperament that is slow to grasp an idea and one that lacks any business acumen or creative drive.

As well as the prominence of the mounts their markings are of particular importance, and a fortune teller will examine these carefully, looking for squares, triangles, stars and crosses, and judging from the positions their individual significance. Squares and triangles are marks of fortune, but stars and crosses are reckoned to be harbingers of bad luck. For example, a square on the Mount of Saturn indicates that the subject will be free of money problems, but a star on the same mount points to the threat of tragedy. A triangle on the Mount of Luna promises success, but a cross there indicates that travel may be risky. A palmist will take all these into consideration before moving to the lines on the palm itself and the study of chiromancy.

There are three main lines etched into every palm: the Heart Line, the Head Line and the Life Line. These supply the core of information in chiromancy, modified and augmented by the many other lines on the palm. So let's deal with these three first.

Heart Line
The depth of this line is a clear indication of the strength of a subject's feelings and emotional drive. When the Heart Line is unbroken it shows a happy and stable marriage. The lower it comes on the palm the greater the sexual impetus and sex-appeal. However, if the line finishes way below the Mount of Jupiter, without rising at the end, this is a sign of reserve and shyness. Similarly a

The Principal Lines of the Left Hand

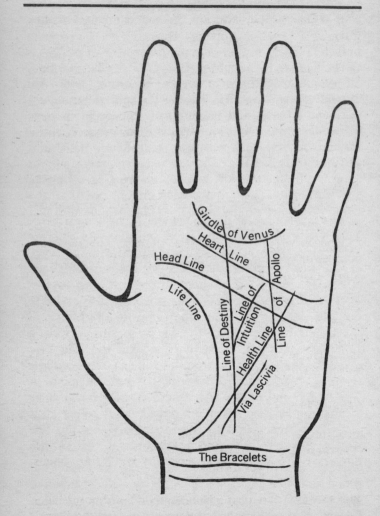

fork at the end of the line can indicate too great a self-absorption, especially if one branch of the fork points towards the Mount of Saturn. Romances are indicated by little lines branching off the Heart Line. Happy ones branch upwards, sadder ones point down.

The balance between the Heart Line and Head Line is an important indicator of emotional control. When the two run side by side it's safe to reckon that the head holds the reins, but when the Heart Line is set high in the palm it means that the head is ruled by the heart. If the two are linked by a third line, this can be read as a mark of a powerful infatuation.

Head Line

The Head Line reflects intellect, with intellectual capacity being matched by length. In general terms a short Head Line indicates limited intellectual horizons. As with the Heart Line, the depth of this line is all-important. A deep, clearly pronounced line indicates great powers of mental application and concentration. In contrast, two parallel lines demonstrate a mind that has trouble deciding what to do. The nearer the Head Line slopes to the Mount of Luna the greater emphasis there is on sensitivity, while a Head Line running in conjunction with the Life Line expresses caution and control. A small gap between these two lines marks an independent, but brilliant mind. A fork at the end of the line has an equally encouraging meaning, indicating a well-developed ability to get ideas across, and the nearer to the Mount of Luna this line sweeps, the more pronounced skills become. A fork with three prongs points to great versatility as a further bonus.

Life Line

This is one of the most misunderstood lines on the palm. In spite of popular belief, it does not predict the time of death but merely indicates the subject's strength and stamina; the deeper and clearer the line, the greater these two elements are, and by association the greater is the chance of a long life. A break in the line shows some severe shock to the system brought on perhaps by a serious illness or injury. Even a short Life Line does not necessarily indicate a short life. It simply warns that energy may need to be conserved to avoid over-taxing the body.

A Life Line which originates as a fork of the Head Line shows that whatever vital energy the subject may have will be tempered by caution and a careful weighing up of any consequences, though if the Life Line actually begins on the Mount of Jupiter the key message is one of great ambition.

Line of Destiny
Of all the lines used to predict the future this is probably the most important. Its root will determine the passage of the subject's early life. For instance, a Line of Destiny that starts on the Mount of Venus is a sign of a life nurtured in a loving family, while one that begins at the Life Line may show a rather limited childhood. The point at which the Line of Destiny ends is of equal importance, particularly when it comes to predicting the outcome of the subject's life. A Line of Destiny sweeping towards the Mount of Apollo is a sign of fame and prosperity, but lines coming down from the Line of Destiny point to failure and disappointment.

Line of Intuition
This line is often hard to find, but if it is clearly manifested on a palm it can be taken as a sign of a highly developed sensitivity and may suggest an interest in mysticism and the supernatural. It is also a sign of a nervous disposition.

Line of Apollo

The importance of the Line of Apollo (sometimes called the Sun Line) lies in its unbroken clarity, which is a mark of success and good luck. Should the line be broken at any point it is a warning that success cannot be assured. The Line of Apollo is important for countering many of the signs of ill-fortune that can be found elsewhere in a palm. In spite of this bonus, there is one feature that even the Line of Apollo cannot gainsay, namely a hollow palm, which is a sign of continuing bad luck.

Girdle of Venus

As its name suggests, this line, formed like a loose chain, indicates a very passionate nature and is often read as a sexual indicator.

Health Line

This line does not exist on every palm, but in cases where it cannot be found there is no cause for worry. On the contrary, the absence of a Health Line is a sure sign that the subject will remain in good health throughout his or her life. Broken Health Lines are signs of nervous conditions, and serious illnesses (shown by breaks in the Life Line) often have spurs of the Health Line running towards them. Providing the Health Line itself is clear and constant the chances of recovery remain good.

Via Lasçivia

This appears on soft, fleshy palms more than firm, harder ones. It marks a desire for stimulus and sensual stimulation which can become sinister if the Head Line is weak.

Bracelets

At the bottom of the palm come these three lines running across the wrist. Provided that they are distinct the subject can look forward to health and happiness in the future. If they rise towards the palm, this suggests some intellectual stimulation; if they rise under the Mount of Luna, a strong imagination may be implied. Lines running from the Bracelets to this mount also indicate journeys, while a line leading to the Mount of Apollo apparently heralds a trip to the tropics! A star in the top bracelet is a sign of money waiting to be inherited, but breaks in any of the lines only offer trouble and anxiety.

These bare guidelines give some indication of the depth and complexity of Romany palmistry, much of which can be divined by an expert in a matter of minutes. Novices require rather longer, and since subjects soon get tired of sitting holding their palms steady, the use of handprints, made either on a photocopier or with traditional ink and roller, are ideal for learning the ropes and putting the techniques into practice.

Practising on your own palm is not considered a useful way to learn. You either know too much about yourself already or you have got used to covering some of the less fortunate sides of your character and may subconsciously (or even consciously) refuse to recognize these in your palm. So it's far more satisfactory to concentrate on palms you don't know anything about.

CHAPTER 6

Left Handicaps

Thirty years ago it was commonly believed that stuttering was a direct result of efforts to change a naturally left-handed child into a right-hander. This had led to a 'hands-off' policy in which most left-handed children were allowed to write, brush their teeth and perform most other manual tasks with their preferred hand. Parents and teachers may still have looked on the practice with some misgiving, but their understanding of the evidence was that all attempts to change the child to the 'normal' way of doing things was almost certain to compound his or her handicap by introducing a speech impediment. Then came the news that this belief was all wrong and that there was no connection between stuttering and changing children from left to right, which resulted in a certain amount of switching again taking place. Today the position is less categorical, and most specialists agree that there may be some connection between left-handedness and speech impediments, while acknowledging that other factors have an equally important part to play.

As mentioned earlier, research has indicated that there may be a link between handedness and man's ability to speak, thanks to the connection between the right hand and the left hemisphere of the brain, which in all right-handers and a good many left-handers appears to control the speech faculty. So it would seem only natural to look for a similar link between left-handedness and some speech difficulties.

From the research undertaken there has been some agreement that stuttering frequently occurs in children before the age of six; that it is found more often in boys than in girls; and that it is also linked in some cases with delays in learning to speak. This pre-six period also marks the time when children establish their hand preferences, revealing a parallel in time as well as in brain sidedness.

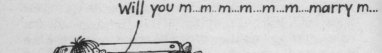

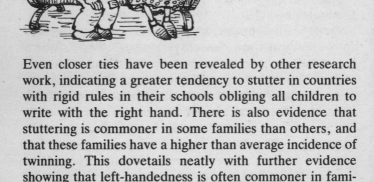

Even closer ties have been revealed by other research work, indicating a greater tendency to stutter in countries with rigid rules in their schools obliging all children to write with the right hand. There is also evidence that stuttering is commoner in some families than others, and that these families have a higher than average incidence of twinning. This dovetails neatly with further evidence showing that left-handedness is often commoner in families which reveal a history of both stuttering and twinning.

Unfortunately this evidence has led to a commonly held but false conclusion that there is an automatic connection between left-handedness and stuttering.

In fact, it need not be left-handedness alone that causes stuttering. The lack of dominant handedness brought about by efforts to switch hands at a vitally impressionable age can apparently be just as serious. An American researcher, Edward Lee Travis, was one of the strongest proponents of this idea just over fifty years ago, when he produced evidence to show that, in American schools at least, the majority of stutterers were left-handers who had been obliged to switch to using the right hand. In Travis's words, 'Their acquired "motor facility" is out of harmony with their native psychological lead'. So they stuttered!

The time at which the attempted switch was made seems to be important too. Evidence suggested that children developed stutters at two crucial periods: when they first began to talk, and when they started to read and write. In the first case this was interpreted as a connection between a delay in learning to speak and developing a clear preference for one hand or the other. The second is related to learning to write, perhaps with the non-dominant hand.

Faced with arguments like these the solution seemed obvious. All that was needed, it appeared, was to switch the stutterers back to using their left hands and their problems would evaporate. In almost every case the authors of these studies were at pains to point out the error of taking such a simplistic view of a vastly more complicated subject. Unfortunately their warnings were largely ignored and in the eyes of a good many less informed readers stuttering was evidently caused by a forced change and could be cured just as easily by allowing the child to revert to the preferred hand.

One of the crucial factors that such a two-dimensional approach ignores is the methods used to change a child's hand. Today it is commonly felt that if a child can be instructed to use the right hand at an early age *without threat or constant pestering*, and provided that the child is happy with the arrangement, then there is nothing to be lost and a great deal to be gained. After all, there's no getting away from the fact that we live in a right-handed world, so that any child who can happily adapt to using the right hand will obviously be relieved of the many minor irks and frustrations of left-handedness which feature elsewhere in the book.

That said it is also acknowledged today that *forcing* a child to become right-handed, or to adopt the right hand as the preferred hand, can be a disastrous policy that may not lead automatically to stuttering, but might affect a child's important early years at school.

A closer examination of the stuttering phenomenon reinforces the argument against a direct hand-switching link. Stuttering is usually associated with nervousness, introspection, embarrassment and a dislike of speaking in public. These in turn aggravate the condition and often result in the stutterer avoiding company and withdrawing more and more into himself. However, from results gained from a study of stuttering in adults who have been cured, and children who stutter at an early age, it appears that these 'symptoms' are not in fact inherent in a stutterer from the outset but build up gradually as a result of the experiences of trying to cope in a non-stuttering world. For a child these problems can be accentuated by well-meaning adults who deliberately spare him the embarrassment of having to speak out in front of others; this may spare the child's feelings in the short term, but has the additional effect of highlighting his 'handicap' even more. As a result the stutter is likely to be made worse, and in these circumstances switching from one hand to the other probably plays very little part in the process.

It's fairly safe to conclude nowadays that a well-managed switch from left to right need have no adverse effect on a child's speech. If the child is strongly left-handed (and there aren't that many who are rigidly biased in favour of one hand or the other) then any responsive teacher or parent will quickly see the danger signals and gently steer the child back to the preferred left hand.

At the same time it does seem sensible to time the switch so as to avoid one of the important phases in the child's life, when he is either making his first efforts to speak or later on is learning to read and write. In other words, children should be encouraged to establish their hand dominance as early as possible, avoiding these critical times.

If a child does start to stutter the chances are that a change of handedness (if that has recently taken place) is only one of a number of important contributory factors.

Here again speech therapists, trained to deal with cases like this, can offer practical help and reassurance.

Observing a child's hand preference at an early age will later be a great help when he or she gets to the stage of starting to write. The first sign parents get of a hand preference is from eating or playing, when the dominant hand will be the one used to pick up a spoon or toy. This can be tested gently by placing objects in the other hand to see if they are switched to the dominant one. Once a preference has been recognized, you at least know where you are when it comes to deciding whether or not to effect a switch. Teachers will help here if asked, and the whole process can be carried out painlessly, and most importantly with understanding and tact.

Many of the problems associated with left-handedness in the past resulted from an overbearing attitude in the classroom which compelled left-handed children to conform and chastised them when they either failed to do so or produced untidy work as a result. We like to think that things have changed today, and certainly there can be few schools in which children are ridiculed or punished for writing with their left hands, though there is still the risk that a busy, harassed teacher may not have the time constantly to help a left-handed writer, particularly if he or she is a right-hander and has no personal experience of the problems the child faces. Parents can help here. A little practice writing with your left hand after the child has gone to bed will soon highlight the snags faced in the classroom. Writing is such a vital skill to master at an early age that time spent in help and encouragement is invaluable both on a practical level and as a confidence-booster; because when all is said and done, it will probably require greater effort from a left-handed child to learn to write clearly and fluidly than from his or her classmates.

When we talk of writing, of course, most of us think automatically of writing from left to right, the direction in which the European languages are written, along with a good many others around the world. However, Semitic languages like Arabic and Hebrew are written in the opposite direction, though Arabic certainly consists of letters which can be written with the right hand far more easily than most Roman letters can be written with the left.

At one time, Greek, from which so much of our current linguistic heritage stems, was also written from right to left. The Etruscans wrote in the same way 750 years before Christ. Then the Greeks started to have other ideas. At one time they even wrote in the *boustrophedon* ('ox-turn') way, in which one line was written from right to left, the next from left to right, the third from right to left, and so on down the page with lines alternating in direction like an ox and plough making its way from side to side across a field. It was only during the 5th century B.C. that Greek writing finally settled down into a fixed left-right pattern which led the way for the rest of Europe. Once again the Greeks had made life difficult for left-handers, just as they had with their attitude towards augury.

Languages written from left to right favour the right-hander without question, and this too may have had some bearing on their development. When writing with pen and ink it is certainly easier to pull the pen than to push it, as so many left-handed writers are obliged to do. Additionally, as the left hand moves across the page it not only covers what has been written but runs the risk of smudging the still wet ink. The arrival of the biro and fast-drying ball and fibre pens has eliminated the latter problem, but the first is harder to deal with.

In the past, left-handed children taught to write with dip pens and ink had a terrible time. To begin with the ink-well was invariably on the right-hand side of the desk which meant that to refill his pen the child had to stretch right across the page and desk. Then the nib, designed for a right-hander, would dig into the paper as the left-hander tried to push it across the page. And the final misery came when the child's hand moved over what had just been written and smudged it all. The whole process was a nightmare.

In an effort to overcome these problems left-handers developed styles of writing which avoided these pitfalls but led to others. One way of allowing the writer to read what he or she has just written is to adopt the hook position, in which the left hand is held above the line of writing and the pen faces inwards towards the body. The position is more awkward than other left-handed ones and as a result can often lead to aching muscles in only a short time. Other common 'faults' developed by left-handed writers are holding the paper at right-angles to the table and consequently writing in towards the body, or placing the paper too far to the right and cramping the writing arm against the body at the end of the line.

The most important aspect to be remembered when writing with the left hand is that it is not the same as writing with the right with the hand simply reversed. If this were the case the writing would move from right to left, with the hand moving away from the body as the line progressed. In fact, left-handed writing requires a different approach.

The position of the paper has an important part to play in the development of a comfortable, fluid, legible left-handed style. In order to prevent squeezing the writing arm against the body at the end of a line, the paper needs to be positioned to the left of centre, giving the arm room to move inwards as the hand reaches the end of the line. The right hand should also be used to hold the page and prevent it from slipping, or in an exercise book from being pushed up by the movement of the left hand. And as the writing gets down to the bottom of the sheet, the paper should be pushed up the desk to make room for the arm and once more prevent any cramping or restriction.

The problem of the obscured line of writing can be overcome if the child is encouraged to hold the pen higher up the stem than he or she might naturally do. If the grip is light this will also relieve tension and help in the formation of clear, rounded letters. Practice with a large crayon on big sheets of paper can be fun and helps to encourage relaxed, fluid writing. This can be a relief too after a day's writing in school worrying about producing neat, tidy writing like the rest of the class, and far from being harmful it can improve this more formal writing by giving confidence and developing balance in the hand.

The transition from crayon or pencil to pen and ink is now nothing like the trauma of days gone by. Today there are several pens on the market designed for left-handers (*Anything Left Handed*, the specialist left-handers' shop – see page 124 – carry an extensive range of left-handed pens, as do many good stationers'). Equipped with one of these, and well drilled beforehand, there is no reason why a left-handed child shouldn't write as neatly and clearly as the right-handers in the class.

One curious characteristic of some left-hand writers is their ability to produce mirror-writing, sometimes quite spontaneously. Mirror-writing is that form of script which appears normal when it is reflected in a mirror. Read on the page in the usual way the letters appear reversed and the script runs from right to left.

Evidence suggests that children are more likely to

produce mirror-writing than adults, and those with sub-normal ability tend to produce it more than children with normal educational capacities. This isn't always the case, mind you; Lewis Carroll, an Oxford maths don as well as the ingenious inventor of dozens of word and number puzzles, not to mention the creator of *Alice in Wonderland* and *Alice Through the Looking Glass*, wrote mirror-script letters to his young friends, and Leonardo da Vinci, whose genius needs no elaboration, kept his notebooks in mirror-writing because, some scholars claim, he found it relaxing after a hard day in the studio!

During the 19th century, doctors began to link mirror-writing with a form of stroke that affected one half of the brain and the opposite side of the body. Cases have also been reported of adults producing mirror-writing while drunk or under the influence of drugs. In searching for an explanation, experts have suggested that mirror-writing may be an intuitive response to being allowed to write freely, in contrast to the strict concentration required in copying school writing exercises or slavishly following a teacher's instructions. Relieved of the inhibiting factor of a copy-book or a teacher's critical gaze, a left-handed child might automatically put into practice hand-writing instructions given earlier *but* in the most natural and comfortable way, which for a left-hander is moving from right to left. This, it is suggested, accounts for the ease with which many left-handers produce mirror-writing, a fact borne out by tests conducted under hypnosis in which adults have been induced to write in this way. (Apparently it can also be achieved as a result of trying to write with both hands simultaneously.)

Another line of argument suggests that mirror-writing is connected with an inability to read; in other words the child writes in this way without realizing that there is anything wrong with it. This idea no doubt lends weight to the conjecture that mirror-writing is associated with backwardness. Children who rely more on the 'feel' of a particular action as opposed to its 'appearance' could understandably go through what appeared to be the motions of normal writing without appreciating that what they were writing was entirely reversed. If they were to write with the right hand the 'feel' would be the same but the results would be normal. The reason that mirror-writing is produced in these circumstances is that the children are attempting to follow their inclinations with the left hand and move from right to left as a result.

Children who have switched to writing with the right hand can also produce mirror-writing when allowed to write with the left hand, but once a child has become accustomed to regular practice writing with one hand, even if he or she has been switched from left to right, this pattern will form a sufficient intellectual barrier impeding any tendency to produce mirror-writing.

There are also simple steps a teacher can take to correct any tendency to write in this way. In the first instance marking the left-hand side of a page as the starting point will help to concentrate a child's attention, even when he or she is doodling, though if this should fail, and mirror-writing continues, it's probably best to restrict the child's writing to copying set letters and words until the movement from left to right is stuck firmly in the child's consciousness.

Before leaving this subject, mention must be made of reading difficulties which were once closely connected with left-handedness. In 1906 it was proposed that all children showing dyslexic (word-blindness) tendencies should be taught to be left-handed! This was simply because dyslexics were known to try and read words from back to front and had great trouble in learning to read as a result. Happily this particular scheme never seems to have been put into practice, but it serves as an indication of some of the remarkable speculation that has taken place in connection with left-handedness and all the ills attributed to it.

What does seem likely is that some of the concomitants of left-handedness, in particular those associated with a late development of a dominant hand or eye, may cause simple confusion when the child's eye meets a word on the page. This often leads to the child trying to read the word first one way and then the other until he or she either understands it or gives up. It seems likely too that finger-pointing is a manifestation of this directional dilemma, and many teachers prefer their children to point and move a finger from left to right along a line, in order to acquire the habit of reading this way, in preference to groping blindly around the printed page in a state of growing frustration and despair. It has even been suggested in the case of dyslexia that successful results can be achieved by blanking out one eye and allowing the child to read with the other. Research continues, but the problem is without question more sympathetically understood than it was eighty years ago.

Not that the impression should be given that all attitudes to left-handedness and related educational problems were treated inconsiderately in the past. Two centuries ago Benjamin Franklin wrote the following *Petition to those in charge of Education* as a 'Letter from the Left Hand', which is a fitting way to conclude this survey of the principal 'handicaps' that have been blamed on the left hand:

I address myself to all the friends of youth and conjure them to direct their compassionate regard to my unhappy fate, in order to remove the prejudices of which I am the victim. There are twin sisters of us; the two eyes of man do not more resemble, nor are capable of being upon better terms with each other than my sister and myself, were it not for the partiality of our parents, who made the most injurious distinction between us. From my infancy I have been led to consider my sister as being of a more elevated rank. I was suffered to grow up without the least instruction, while nothing was spared in her education. She had masters to teach her writing, drawing, music and other accomplishments; but if, by chance, I touched a pencil, a pen, or a needle, I was bitterly rebuked; and more than once I have been beaten for being awkward and wanting a graceful manner. It is true my sister associated with me upon some occasions; but she always made a point of taking the lead, calling upon me from necessity, or to figure by her side.

But conceive not, sirs, that my complaints are instigated merely by vanity. No, my uneasiness is occasioned by an object much more serious. It is the practice of our family, that the whole business of providing for its subsistence falls upon my sister and myself. If any indisposition should attack my sister – and I mention it in confidence, upon this occasion that she is subject to gout, the rheumatism, and cramp, without making mention of other accidents – what would be the fate of our poor family? Must not the regret of our parents be excessive, at having placed so great a difference between sisters who are so perfectly equal? Alas! We must perish from distress; for it would not be in my power even to scrawl a suppliant petition for relief, having been obliged to employ the hand of another in transcribing the request which I have now the honour to prefer to you.

Condescend, sir, to make my parents sensible of the injustice of an exclusive tenderness, and of the necessity of distributing their care and affection among all their children equally.

I am, with profound respect, Sirs,

> Your obedient servant,
>
> The Left Hand.

CHAPTER 7

It's All Right to be Left

Any left-hander feeling down-trodden and hard done by has only to look to Leonardo da Vinci, the world's most famous sinistral, to draw comfort and inspiration. Leonardo was born illegitimate, which in some circles would have automatically branded him with the Bend Sinister on his heraldic arms, if he had had any, as a mark of bastardy. His grandfather lamented his left-handedness because of its close associations with the devil and his works. Yet in spite of these setbacks he became established as the greatest creative genius of the Middle Ages, and almost the personification of the Renaissance itself.

He was the complete man in every intellectual if not emotional sense. His writing ranged over philosophy, art, music, medicine, architecture, poetry, physics, religion and geology. As an inventor he was far ahead of his time. Apart from designing scissors and lock-gates, which had immediate practical application for his contemporaries, he drew up plans for what amounted to helicopters and aeroplanes, parachutes, sub-aqua equipment, subterranean communications systems, a submarine and high-explosive bombs. He also produced the largest book in mirror-writing in the world, in which he jotted down most of these ideas and schemes after a busy day creating the *Mona Lisa* or some other masterpiece. As his biographer Giorgio Vasari noted, Leonardo 'wrote backwards, in rude characters, and with the left hand, so that anyone who is not practised in reading them cannot understand them'. He could also write with one hand while he was drawing with the other.

Many artists at that time were known to be ambidextral, Michelangelo being perhaps the most famous. However, studies of Leonardo's work show that he apparently never drew with his right hand. This may have been used for painting, though to relieve fatigue it was probably alternated with the left, but for most other purposes Leonardo appears to have been left-handed and proud of it.

Questions have been posed however as to whether he was naturally a left-hander or one by adoption. These ideas have arisen from suggestions that his right hand might have been crippled or damaged as a result of a brawl, and from contemporary accounts of his having difficulty in using it. The mystery remains unsolved, but to all practical purposes Leonardo was a sinistral. A study of his mechanical inventions, for instance, reveals that most cranks included in the designs could only have been operated by the left hand.

Other left-handed artists have included Hans Holbein the Younger, who made his name at the court of Henry VIII and painted many of the most famous people of the Tudor age, as well as including a number of unmistakeably left-handed figures in the *Dance of Death* series; Paul Klée, the pioneer of much modern art; and Pablo Picasso, one of its greatest exponents. The German painter and illustrator, Adolf von Menzel, who flourished during the reign of Frederick the Great, was totally ambidextral and once admitted: '. . . when I paint in oils, I always use my right hand; for drawings, aquarelles, and gouaches, always the left . . . No one is able to tell with which hand I have worked, and to me it makes no difference.' This revealing comment supports a popular idea that the left 'nd, and the right side of the brain that controls it, is responsible for creating the initial shape and structure of a work of art and is in some mysterious way closest to an artist's (in fact everyone's) instinctive being.

Against this must be balanced an anecdote told of Sir Edward Landseer, Queen Victoria's painting tutor, who like his royal pupil was also ambidextrous. Landseer was at a reception at which the suggestion was made that no one could draw two different subjects, one with each hand, at the same time. There was general agreement that this was impossible until Landseer confounded everyone by doing just that. He sat down at a writing desk with a pencil in each hand and simultaneously drew the head of a dog with one hand and a stag's head with the other. When asked to compare them no one present could claim that one was inferior to the other!

Handedness itself is also believed to be a factor in the creation of much Western art. In the vast majority of all great paintings, drawings and watercolours, the focal point lies on the right, and whether consciously or unconsciously artists tend to centre the aspect of greatest visual attention here. The action of paintings of this type invariably moves to the right. If a figure is painted on the left, the eyes, hands or other organs of movement are directed to the right. And when the direction is reversed and the action and visual direction veer to the left, this comes as a considerable shock to the system. Perhaps this is connected with our habit of reading from left to right. Perhaps it says something about the basic visual and interpretative instincts of Western man that we expect to 'read' a painting in this way; in contrast, much Oriental art focuses attention to the left. Whatever the reason, a close analysis of almost any Western canvas, or sculpture even, will demonstrate a subtle relationship between left and right.

Heinrich Woelfflin, a distinguished art historian, made a detailed study of this phenomenon and came up with some striking results. He examined an etching by Rembrandt called *The Three Trees* and compared it with its mirror image. In the original the three trees stand to the right of centre. The area to the left of centre is filled with a distant landscape, and in the top left-hand corner is a dark triangle of cloud or rain that highlights the light sky behind the trees. In the mirror image the picture is of course reversed and the visual effect is dramatic. The focal point now becomes the landscape, deep and broad, stretching away to the right. The trees now stand on the left of the picture and seem almost incidental to the main dramatic thrust centred on the landscape.

A similar result was achieved by producing a mirror-image of Degas's painting *The Millinery Shop*. Here again the focal point of the original is a woman sitting on the right of the picture, holding a hat out to the right in her right hand and making some alteration to it with her left. The centre and left side of the picture contain other hats, one lying on the table, the others on stands arranged on the table. If the picture is turned round and its mirror-image studied, the woman has moved to the left. The hat she holds and her attention, as well as our own, are directed towards the left. The hats in the right of the picture seems to dominate the canvas, no doubt because our eyes are conditioned to concentrating on that area. The attention drawn to the left seems unnatural and is resisted.

Switching to another artistic medium, music this time, we find that again the left hand is frequently the loser. Prokofiev and Benjamin Britten both wrote piano concertos for the left hand but the one which has aroused the greatest interest among left-handed pianists is the D

Major concerto composed by Ravel for his friend Paul Wittgenstein, the Austrian pianist who had lost his right hand in the Great War. Wittgenstein found it a great challenge and had to hand the piece over to someone else after the first performance; he subsequently didn't play it again for some time until his confidence had been restored. The critics gave it a rough time too. But in the eyes of all left-handers it is a landmark in understanding and sympathy; not so much for the music that Ravel wrote but for the dedication that went on the outside of the score:

> This is not so much to show what the left hand can do, but to prove what can be done for the appendage that suffers from sinistral stigma.

Few left-handers could have phrased it better, and the remark is all the more heartening coming from a composer who was a confirmed right-hander himself.

Music is one of the few disciplines in which being a left-hander is not always a disadvantage. It is said that the French horn, for instance, requires greater dexterity in the left hand than in the right. The violin, however, presents a different picture. This is invariably built and strung to be played by a right-hander on the left shoulder, using the right hand to control the bow. Playing from the right shoulder, as did the left-handed violinist Charlie Chaplin, requires more than a simple change in the order of the strings. Internal adjustments are required to maintain correct resonance; and the chin rest also has to be changed. Even if the alterations were generally practicable, imagine the confusion that would be caused in an orchestra if a left-handed violinist sat among an otherwise dextral string section. While they would all be happily sawing away with their bows to the left, the left-hander would be moving in the opposite direction towards them.

Even if clashes could be avoided the effect on the conductor would be very distracting.

Similarly with the guitar, even fairly straightforward alterations are not really as practical as they seem. While some cheaper guitars can probably be re-strung for left-handed players, more expensive ones certainly require additional alterations to ensure the same quality of sound, and in most cases manufacturers of instruments like these build special left-handed guitars from the outset.

Left-handed guitarists represent some of the few truly left-handed musicians. The late Jimi Hendrix and Paul McCartney are two famous examples of sinistrals who have made it to the top in a right-handed world.

In most cases children, right-handers and left-handers alike, are taught to play musical instruments in the right-handed way. This isn't as unfair or extreme as it sounds. As most teachers point out, picking up a musical instrument is a fairly unnatural action for any child, and he or she will need to be taught how to hold it and how to control the stops or strings before any sounds can be produced. Whether a child is right- or left-handed makes almost no difference at this stage, and since most instruments are made to be played in a particular manner there is no sense of discrimination one way or the other.

Charlie Chaplin, the world's most popular left-handed violinist, is also a convenient example of the strongest apparent link between left-handedness and creativity at performance level. Think for a moment of the number of famous comedians who are or were left-handers: W. C. Fields, Harpo Marx, Lennie Bruce, Richard Pryor, Kenneth Williams, George Burns, and Chaplin himself, to mention only a few. Then come the actors and film stars: Robert de Niro, Marilyn Monroe, Judy Garland, Olivia de Havilland, Rod Steiger, Telly Savalas, Rex Harrison, Shirley Maclaine, Marcel Marceau, Rock Hudson, Kim Novak, Greta Garbo and Betty Grable. These names alone indicate a higher than average number of top stars who are left-handed.

Shifting our attention to another level of performance, the world of professional tennis, the list is just as impressive. Jimmy Connors, Bjorn Borg, John McEnroe, Rod Laver, Manuel Orantes, Guillermo Vilas, and Martina Navratilova among others constitute about 40 per cent of the world's leading tennis players, and they are all left-handers. This must lend encouragement if for no other reason than the fact that tennis as played at the top level is a game requiring a remarkable combination of power and skill. For the left hand, so long the subordinate, to shine in this most exacting of manual skills must be an inspiration to all left-handers facing their own private struggles.

Perhaps the most 'public' of private struggles also benefited from a game of tennis. This was the fate of King George VI, a changed left-hander who struggled to adapt to using his right hand and developed a stutter into the bargain. After a fairly wretched childhood this particular left-hander finally made good as a tennis player of no mean achievement. After winning the RAF Doubles he received a telegram from no lesser person than the King himself, congratulating his son on his victory. In 1924 the Duke of York appeared in the Wimbledon championships, the first and so far only member of the royal family to do so. He and his doubles partner were knocked out in the first round without winning a set, but in the eyes of the public at least the young, stuttering prince had proved himself an unquestionable success when allowed to use his left hand in his own way. (There's more than a touch of irony in his elder brother's later decision to forgo a 'left-handed' (morganatic) marriage to Mrs Simpson and lose the crown in the process, thus landing his unsuspecting brother with the throne.)

In cricket, left-handers have always been on an equal footing with right-handers, and frequently achieve considerable success as a result of being slightly 'unusual'. A left-handed bowler, for example, can approach the pitch and bowl 'around' the wicket at an angle that a right-handed bowler could never achieve, whereas a left-handed batsman requires a change of field when he is at the striking end and as a result can delay the progress of the game for a strategic period by running singles with a right-hander and making the fielders cross from one side of the pitch to the other time after time. Many a draw has been forced by tactics like this. One of the curious features of many left-hand bowlers is that they become right-hand batsmen, although this wasn't actually the case with perhaps the greatest left-handed cricketer of all time, Sir Gary Sobers, who batted and bowled left-handed.

Other notable sporting left-handers have been Mark Spitz, the astonishing American swimmer who won seven Olympic gold medals in 1972; Babe Ruth, the baseball star who hit a record total of 714 home runs which remained unequalled until 1974, and who made over two million dollars from the game between 1914 and 1935; and another American, Ben Hogan the golfer, who played right-handed because he was told that his stroke would improve by using the greater strength in his leading arm, and who became USPGA champion in 1946 and 1948, US Open champion in 1948, 1950, 1951 and 1953, world champion in 1951 and 1953, Open champion in 1953, and Masters champion in 1951 and 1953. All of these titles after 1949 were won despite the serious injuries Hogan received in a car accident that year. His struggle back to the top is one of the great stories of golf.

There have also been three left-handed US presidents: James Garfield, Harry Truman and Gerald Ford, though the latter plays golf, throws a ball and writes on a blackboard with his right hand. In British politics, Roy Jenkins and Gerald Kaufmann are two notable left-handers.

But just in case right-handers feel that too much emphasis is being given to sinistral success stories, left-handers should remember that both Billy the Kid and Jack the Ripper were left-handed!

CHAPTER 8

Side by Side by Testing

According to *The New England Journal of Medicine*, there's an easy way of telling whether or not you are left-handed. All you need do is to look at your thumbnails. If the base of the left nail is broader and squarer than the right, then you're left-handed.

Not every researcher would agree with this particular test and over the years left-handers have been subjected to a wide range of examinations with the object of discovering what makes them tick. If you want to try a few of them out for yourself, here is a selection you might like to try.

Blau Test
This was developed by an American researcher, Theodore Blau, who asked his subjects to draw crosses and then circle them, using each hand in turn. According to his thesis those who draw the circles anti-clockwise are left-handed.

Van Riper Critical Angle Board
This test, with its awe-inspiring name, was designed fifty years ago by an American therapist, Van Riper. He set out to produce a reliable test that concentrated on high-lighting laterality in various degrees. The test that resulted was one that involved simultaneous drawing of an asymmetrical pattern with both hands, on opposite sides of a vertical board. From this developed the more sophisti-

cated variant in which the boards could be rotated through 90 degrees to test degrees of laterality.

The test begins with the vertical boards parallel with the subject's chest and set at chest height. The subject is then asked to copy an asymmetric diagram mounted in front of the apparatus and slightly above eye-level. The copying must be made with both hands at the same time, one hand copying on to one board, one on to the other. The subject must copy the diagram as quickly as possible and must keep his or her eyes on it the whole time.

Once the first drawing has been made the paper is wound on to a fresh sheet on each board and the boards are moved round by 10 degrees. Then the test is repeated exactly as before. This procedure progresses stage by stage, with the angle increasing by 10 degrees each time. This gradual angling makes the task more difficult and at some stage the subject is likely to draw a mirror image of the diagram with one hand. When this happens the examiner notes the angle and tries one further 10-degree movement to confirm this. The angle at which the mirroring occurs is known as the critical angle, by which Van Riper hoped to prove degrees of handedness. In the cases where the boards eventually came back to back without any mirroring taking place he concluded that the subjects were truly ambidextrous. In all other cases mirroring occurred somewhere in the non-dominant hand. He even went as far as suggesting that left-handers who had switched to writing with their right hands might still mirror with the right hands under these conditions, since the intrinsic dominance of the left hand would shine through.

Cross Test
This amounts to a variation of Theodore Blau's test and involves writing four sets of crosses in a set period, say

half-a-minute, two with the right hand, two with the left. The subject is asked to write one set with one hand as fast as possible in the set time, then change hands and repeat the test. This process is completed twice and the totals will reveal the speed with which the subject uses both hands, the faster hand being the dominant one.

Screw Test
A test of handedness in simple manual tasks, this concentrates on the hand preferred for unscrewing and screwing bottle tops or jar lids. Again speed is emphasized and the subject is asked to remove all the tops and replace them as quickly as possible. Again the dominant hand will be the one that actually removes the tops, rather than holds the jars or bottles.

Reaching Test
When asked to reach energetically for something most people will instinctively stretch out their dominant hands,

and in this test the subject is made to sit in a chair while the examiner holds an object above his or her head just within reaching distance and mid-way between the two hands so that there is no bias to one side or the other. On command the subject has to reach up with *one* hand to try and touch the object. This is repeated several times with the object being raised slightly each time. Again the dominant hand should be the one the subject prefers to stretch up with.

Throwing test

This simple test only works correctly if no suggestion is made as to which hand the subject should use. The subject can either throw the ball to the examiner or at a target – a bucket perhaps. When the ball is returned, he or she should be allowed to select the hand with which to throw. Only after a clear preference has been established should the subject be asked to throw the ball with the non-dominant hand to see how proficient that is. Again, if no marked preference is shown for either hand the subject is largely ambidextrous.

General preference test

This is based on a test created by R. C. Oldfield and described in an article that appeared in the *British Journal of Psychology* in February 1969 under the title *Handedness in Musicians*. Subjects were asked to state their hand preference for the following, so you might enjoy having a try at it yourself. (Place a tick under LEFT for a left preference, and one under RIGHT for a right preference.)

LEFT   *RIGHT*

Writing

Drawing

Throwing

Scissors

Razor

Comb

Toothbrush

Knife (without fork)

Spoon

Hammer

Screwdriver

Tennis racket

Fishing rod

Knife with fork

Cricket bat (lower hand)

Golf club (lower hand)

Broom (upper hand)

Rake (upper hand)

Striking match (match)

Opening box (lid)

Dealing cards (cards being dealt)

Threading needle (needle or thread according to which is *moved*)

Which foot do you prefer to kick with?

Which eye do you use when only using one?

If the majority of ticks appear on one side that is your dominant one. If the number is even then you can reckon yourself to be ambidextrous.

CHAPTER 9

Life on the Left Side

Left-handers are clumsy, claim the majority of right-handers. Observation confirms it. You've only got to see a left-hander trying to use a pair of scissors, pour milk from a saucepan, wind a wristwatch, or use a corkscrew to prove the point.

That just about sums up the typical dextral attitude to sinistrals, who for centuries, if not millennia, have laboured under the grim knowledge that one thing they can never be is dextrous in the true sense of the word. The reason is pathetically simple. Only when left-handed implements started to appear did the problems begin evaporating overnight.

Give a right-hander a pair of left-handed scissors and see how he copes. Ask him to sign his name with a left-handed pen and see who the joke's on then. Experience has shown that once left-handers are provided with equipment designed to suit their needs they are every bit as 'dextrous', if not more so, than most right-handers. For one thing, their subordinate hand, the right one, is usually far more efficient than the left hand of most dextrals, simply because left-handers have had to get used to using it so often.

This 'handicap' exists in most avenues of daily life. At work, left-handed craftsmen face infuriating problems trying to work at benches and lathes designed for right-handers. On some extreme occasions left-handers have even been advised to go and find work elsewhere because of the problems they faced and the poor productivity that resulted. Left-handed dentists can now buy a complete left-handed surgery with chair and implements suited to their needs. Barbers and hairdressers can buy left-handed scissors to help them in their work, though the majority of hairdryers even a few years ago were operated more easily in the right hand. It is still true that many specialist tools for the left-hander, in a wide range of skills, are still hard to find.

Scissors have always been a particular annoyance to the sinistral, especially in childhood, when one of the greatest pleasures is cutting out paper shapes. For a comparatively simple tool the scissor has presented an insurmountable problem for the left-hander. In a right-handed scissor, when cutting anything but the easiest material, the upper

blade is pushed towards the lower one by the action of the fingers pushing the blade in towards the body, while the thumb pushes the lower blade away from the body. The result is that the two cutting edges are forced together and meet accurately as they cut. Now put the same scissor in the left hand and the action is reversed. The blades are pushed apart and hard as you try they refuse to cut anything but the thinnest material. This is the problem the left-hander has always faced with scissors. So what, you might think?

The answer is it matters a great deal when you are at playgroup or just having fun at home. While your right-handed friends are having a high old time cutting out bits of paper and doing clever things with their scissors, yours obstinately refuse to cut as neatly and precisely. Frustration, anger and despair soon set in. Extreme as the argument may be, if this very early step in education is stymied by what appears to be an inability to perform the simplest task that everyone else does without thinking, what are the prospects for the child who has soon to cope with far more testing skills, the most daunting of which is wielding a pen? Luckily that particular problem has long since been solved by the ready availability of left-handed scissors. But it still requires that imaginative effort on the part of the parents or teacher to spot a left-handed child early enough to introduce a pair of suitable scissors and rebuild confidence before it is too late.

Even at later stages of education, left-handers can run into infuriating narrow-mindedness. Take the type of student desk found in many schools and colleges in America. It is designed with one arm specially widened to help the sitter take notes. Which arm is widened? The right one inevitably, leaving left-handed students having to struggle to make notes on their knees, or wobbling uneasily on the narrower left arm. Yes, there are a few of these desks designed for left-handers, but they are few and far between.

Then what about telephones? How many public phone boxes have the receiver mounted on the right, or even in the centre? The answer is as good as none. In most countries the receiver is deliberately placed on the left, allowing the right and more commonly dextrous hand to feed in coins, rummage in pockets for extra ones and jot down messages. When the left-hander goes to use a public coin box the results are hilarious from the outside. He may start confidently enough with the receiver in the left hand, dialling with the right and feeding in the coins, but if he needs to write anything down the fun really starts. The hands are switched. The cable now stretches across his body to the right ear. Out comes the pen and paper in the left hand which then stretches across to the right to find a flat surface on which to write, and with arms crossed and probably with the pips sounding in his ear demanding more money, the wretched left-hander tries to write his note.

Then you go to the bank to sign a cheque, or to the polling booth to cast your vote, and where are the fixed pens and pencils? On the right again. Most cheque books too are printed for right-handers, though at least one enterprising bank in America produces cheque books for left-handed customers so that they don't have to cross hands to hold the stub end steady while they write.

At home the problems can be even more acute. In the kitchen, wall-mounted tin openers are invariably made for right-handers; so are a good many of the ordinary rotary ones used in the hand. Here again left-handed ones are available, but you have to search for them. Potato peelers, kitchen knives, kitchen scissors, saucepans and ladles are utensils which most right-handers use automatically but which require a great deal more skill and concentration when used in the other hand. (You can now buy left-handed versions of these too.)

Irons, too, have come a long way since the days when most of them had the flex attached to the right side of the iron. In the hands of the poor left-hander, the flex would hang between his or her body and the ironing-board, constantly getting in the way. Most ironing boards also had the heat pad on the right and the sheet rail pointing from right to left, a design which resulted in left-handed ironers having to turn the whole thing the other way round. Fortunately times have brought a change at last and left-handers no longer face the prospect of a domestic life in which ironing is more of a drudgery and struggle than it otherwise would be thanks to the vagaries of the iron and the ironing board.

Folding sheets can have its moments too if one folder is dextral the other sinistral. So can laying a table when left-handed children frequently place knives, forks, glasses and everything else 'the wrong way round'. Once the meal is over washing-up can be more tiresome than usual when the left-hander inevitably finds the draining board on the left of the sink; his or her natural inclination is to use the right hand, the subordinate one, to put the washed articles on the board, so a draining board on the right is a boon for left-handers too.

Old-fashioned, hand-operated sewing machines were built with the handle on the right. However, this did leave the left hand free for the more intricate job of feeding through the material, and if a left-hander couldn't cope with the right-hand handle, there were always the foot-operated treadle machines that freed both hands.

When knitting, left-handers knit with the wool and working needle in their left hands. In all other respects the process is the same as for their right-handed colleagues. However, there is a type of continental knitting, similar to crocheting, which actually favours left-handedness. Here the knitter holds needle and wool in her left hand and hooks this through the right-hand needle, an operation which many right-handers would find impossibly fiddly.

The old scissor problem made dressmaking a difficult task until the advent of left-handed pinking shears and dressmaker's scissors put both dextrals and sinistrals on an equal footing. Though even now trousers with only one back pocket, and single pocketed skirts and dressing-gowns, invariably have that pocket on the right, which in

the case of the trousers at least makes it as good as useless to left-handed wearers. (Trouser zips too seem designed exclusively for right-hand use.)

Even the wonders of modern technology haven't escaped this ubiquitous dextral bias. Television knobs, hi-fi knobs, record-player arms, and a good many cameras are designed for right-handed use. This doesn't preclude left-handers, of course, but it does make handling them that little bit more difficult.

Outdoors, left-handers have always had trouble with rifles and shotguns unless they were specifically designed for their use, as were those issued to German left-handed troops during the Second World War. There were many British conscripts, however, left-handers to a man, who suffered constant irritation from the loading and ejection mechanisms on earlier rifles which were naturally geared for right-hand use. While on the topic of soldiers and their training, there are stories told in both Germany and Britain of recruits to either the Kaiser's army or the early Highland regiments who experienced some difficulty in distinguishing between left and right. Since military drill depends on these to a large extent it was vital to drum the lesson in as quickly as possible. The solution arrived at was to tie a bunch of hay to one ankle and a bunch of straw to the other. Then the orders were given 'hay foot . . . straw foot . . . hay foot . . . straw foot . . .' until the penny finally dropped.

Golfers and cricketers, tennis players and boxers seem to fare quite successfully as left-handers, and have produced a far higher proportion of champions than the number of left-handers in general would suggest. In the case of cricket and golf, of course, they have had to find special equipment – a whole bag of left-handed clubs or a cricket glove that gives protection to the left thumb.

Hockey is a different matter. Left-handed hockey sticks do not exist. In the regulation hockey stick, one side of the business end is flat, the other rounded, and the ball may only be struck by the flat side, even when dribbling along the ground. In ice hockey the rules are different and there left-handers have also reached championship level.

In fencing too left-handers have often had the edge! As early as the age of Roman gladiatorial combats left-handers were much in demand with, according to one contemporary account, as many as half the gladiators being southpaws. During training the other half were given special instruction on what to do when up against one of these.

In baseball, where the term *southpaw* originated, left-handed players have certain advantages. After completing his swing a left-handed batter is not only facing towards but moving in the direction of first base, which gives him a head start in running out his hit. On the other side of the coin the left-handed pitcher is able to watch first base during the wind up to his pitch, which is helpful in cutting down the hitter's lead, while the man at first base can use his gloved right hand to cover a large area of the in-field as well as having the advantage of throwing with his left hand to the man at second base. Not many years ago almost half the leading players in this position were left-handers.

The one sport in which being left-handed is a positive disadvantage is polo, because it's actually against the rules to play left-handed! The reason is one of safety to both pony and rider. When a player is challenged for the ball he must play it on his off side, that's to say his right side. The challenger must also play the ball on the off side, ensuring that they meet stick to stick. Were a left-hander to tackle a right-hander from the opposite direction their sticks would be on opposite sides and their ponies would clash head-on. At one time left-handed players were allowed to play provided they were registered as being competent. With the speeding up of the game in recent years left-handed play has been outlawed altogether to remove any risk of injury.

Before leaving horses and the left in everyday life, we ought to cast our minds back to those happy days before the arrival of the internal combustion engine when all road transport relied on horse-power in the true sense. Here, many believe, lies the origin of the side of the road on which we drive – the left in Britain, parts of the Commonwealth and a few countries in Asia, and the right in the rest of the world.

One theory holds that driving on the left was formerly the rule throughout western Europe, in accordance with a papal decree commanding all travellers to ride or drive on the left-hand side of the road for their own safety, so

Still finding difficulty in mounting the horse the British way, Herr Schmidt?

allowing themselves plenty of room on the right side to wield a whip, if the horses or other road users caused trouble. The switch to driving on the right, so this story goes, was brought about in the French Revolution, when Robespierre and the other atheist leaders decided that the left-hand rule of the road was a religious institution and changed over to driving on the right in order to eliminate it.

Another school of thought takes the sitting position of the 'driver' as the determining factor. Left-handed driving in Britain (a country largely free from influences either from Rome or revolutionary Paris), and the countries that followed her lead, seems to have derived from the sitting positions adopted by coachmen and waggoners. They habitually sat on the right side of their vehicles, to allow themselves the freest use of their whips. In this position, they would naturally have pulled over to the left when passing other vehicles, thus allowing both 'drivers' a clear view of what each team of horses was up to. When roads became wider, this manoeuvre gradually became institutionalized as the accepted practice of driving on the left side of the road all the time.

However, in a number of other European countries and, by extension, North America, 'drivers' were accustomed to sitting on the opposite side of their vehicles. They were mainly postillions, who chose to sit on the rear horse on the left-hand side of the team, from where they were in the best position to control all the horses. Seated here, the safest way to pass was by moving over to the right; again allowing both 'drivers' an uninterrupted view as they passed.

So driving on the left can be seen either as a remote vestige of papal sway, or, more likely, the established practice in those countries where 'drivers' habitually sat on the right side of their vehicles. Similarly, driving on the right developed either from post-revolutionary custom in France, or from a general rule in countries where 'drivers' normally sat on the left.

Sweden switched to the right over a decade ago, but the British have stolidly stuck to their traditional left-side driving and look like doing so for the forseeable future. Even the prospect of a road link with Europe didn't deter one inspired British motorist, who wrote to the press with a splendid compromise. Why didn't British drivers stick to the left in the tunnel or on the bridge and Continental drivers keep to the right, he suggested? Little wonder we've been making heavy weather of European co-operation!

As a postscript for anyone interested in acquiring any of the kitchen utensils, pens, garden tools or other left-handed implements referred to earlier, here is the catalogue of that left-hander's Aladdin's cave in London, the shop that every left-hander or parent of a left-handed child should enter in their address book and diary:

> ANYTHING LEFT HANDED
> 65 Beak Street
> London W1R 3LF
> Tel. 01-437 3910

They provide a mail-order service as well as sales over the counter, and will supply up-to-date prices on application.

Beak Street can be reached by tube from either Oxford Circus or Piccadilly Circus Underground stations. From Oxford Circus walk down Regent Street past Liberty's until you find Beak Street leading off to the left; Anything Left Handed is down towards the far end. From Piccadilly Circus walk up Regent Street until you find Beak Street leading off to the right. In either case it's a fairly short walk which will be richly rewarded whether you're after a T-shirt, an Italic pen, a moustache cup or a tin-opener – all of which put the left-hander first for once.

Catalogue

Kitchen & Tableware

Waves Can Opener. One-piece stainless steel cutter. Very robust. Fully LH.

Butterfly Can Opener. Fully LH.

Rotary Can Opener. Swiss precision-made. 1-year guarantee. Removes top of cans leaving a smooth edge. Fully LH.

Lancashire Potato-Peeler. String-bound wooden handle and stainless steel blade. Fully LH.

Potato Peeler. Rigid Blade, plastic handle. Dishwasherproof. Fully LH.

Potato Peeler/Knife. Swivel action peeler with straight edge knife and shredder. A plastic sheath fits over the part not in use to form a handle. A most useful and wellmade implement. LH. and RH.

Corkscrew. Wooden handle, LH thread.

Ladle with LH lip. Stainless steel with wooden handle.

Kitchen Devil Grapefruit Knife. Surgical steel. LH and RH.

Grapefruit Knife. LH cutting edge. Stainless steel, wooden handle.

Kitchen Devil All-purpose Knife. With a device for peeling and slicing. 6″ (150 mm). LH and RH.

Kitchen Devil Knife. Curved blade. 8½″ (220 mm). Ideal for slicing and dicing, also filleting.

Kitchen Devil Cooks' Multi-purpose Knife. Straight edge. 8″ (200 mm).

Kitchen Devil Cook's Carver. Surgical steel. 12″ (300 mm).

Kitchen Devil Sharpener. Will keep all your knives super sharp. LH and RH.

Kleen-Kut Knife. Wide-toothed LH cutting edge. Stainless steel. Wooden handle. 12½" (320 mm), Bread knife, carver or slicer.

Cook's Friend. Broad Palate Knife with wide-toothed LH cutting edge. Stainless steel. Top grade manufacture and finish. 11½.009 (285 mm).

Zest Cutter. A neat implement for cutting citrus rind for flavour or decoration. Steel cutter, plastic grip. Fully LH.

Pastry Slice. All-metal stainless steel. LH cutting edge. In presentation box.

Pastry Slice. LH cutting edge. Wooden handle.

Pie Server. LH cutting edge. Wooden handle.

Expanding Spatula. The three blades of this spatula can be fanned out from the centre by simple thumb pressure. Ideal for serving omelettes, whole fish, etc. from the pan to dish. Stainless steel. Strong.

Butter Spreader. Fully LH. Simple, effective spatula for spreading. Stainless steel, wooden handle. 8" (200 mm).

Tomato Slicer and Lifter. An excellent cutting implement with a widened head for lifting the slices. Stainless steel, wooden handle. 8" (200 mm).

Steak Knife. All-metal. Fully LH. 8" (200 mm).

Steak Knife. Stainless steel, Ivorine handle. 8½" (215 mm).

Steak Knife. As above. 9¼" (235 mm).

Steak Knife. Stainless steel with horn handle. Fully LH. 8" (200 mm).

Pastry Fork. Stainless steel with rosewood handle. 8" (200 mm). Fully LH.

Pastry Fork. Stainless steel. 6" (152 mm). Fully LH.

Spoon. Very elegant LH design in stainless steel. 6½" (165 mm).

'Mouli', Moulinex Herb Master. Chops everything. LH and RH.

Scissors

Child's First Scissor. A fully LH and fully safety scissor for the youngest age groups (2–6). Blunt-on-blunt and round ends. All-metal. 4″ (100 mm). Very robust and recommended for play-groups etc.

Child's scissor. Also for the youngest age groups. Sharp blades, rounded ends. Plastic (red) grips. 4½″ (115 mm). The easiest scissor of all to use but slightly less safe than one above.

'Lefty' Paper scissor. Fully LH. 4″ (100 mm). Plastic (light green) grips. A. Rounded ends B. Blunt Points.

'Lefty' Scissor. For the slightly older (5–9). 5″ (127 mm). Fully LH. Plastic (dark green) grips.

'Lefty' Teaching scissor. With 4-hole plastic grips (2 for child and 2 for mother). Rounded ends. 6½″ (165 mm). Fully LH.

'Lefty' Teaching Scissor. As above with blunt pointed ends. 7½″ (190 mm).

Child's 6″ Scissor (8–12 years). All-metal with plastic lined grips. Fully LH.

Nail scissor. Straight blades 3¾″ (95 mm). By Kutrite of Sheffield. Fully LH.

Nail Scissor. As above. By Taylor's Eye Witness of Sheffield. Fully LH.

Nail Scissors. Two 3½″ (90 mm) scissors, L & R, in a leather case.

Supasnip. This brilliant invention cuts both the L and the R with the same scissor. 4″ (100 mm).

All-Purpose Scissor. Fully LH 8½″ (220 mm). Very comfortable, plastic moulded grips.

All-purpose Scissor. 6″ (155 mm). An elegant scissor

suitable for the office desk. Fully LH. All-metal with plastic-lined grips.

Fiskars Scissor from Wilkinson. The G.P. Scissor. 8″ (200 mm). LH grips on RH blades.

Fiskars Kitchen Scissor from Wilkinson. LH grips. 7½ (190 mm).

Dressmakers' Lightweight Scissor. By WISS. Fully LH. 8″ (200 mm). All-metal with coated grips.

Mundial All-Purpose Scissor. A superb scissor for dressmaking and paper. Fully LH. Plastic moulded grips.

Dressmakers' Scissor, Sheffield. With side bents. By Kutrite. Fully LH. 8½″ (220 mm). All-metal with coated grips.

Embroidery Scissor. Sheffield. Fully LH. 3½″ (90 mm).

Dressmakers' Scissor. The Mundial Serra Sharp. 8½″ (220 mm). An all-metal scissor with side bents and coated grips.

Pinking Shear. Fully LH. All-metal. 8½″ (220 mm). Very strong, suitable for tailor's work.

Pinking Shear. By Mundial. All-metal. 7½″ (190 mm). Very easy in action.

All-purpose Scissor. Small. A very convenient all-metal traditional scissor. Italian. 6″ (155 mm). Fully LH.

All-purpose Scissor. Medium. All-metal traditional scissor. Italian. 7″ (180 mm). Fully LH.

Small Dressmakers' Scissor. All-metal. 7″ (180 mm). Perhaps the sharpest scissor in the world. Fully LH.

Tailors' Shears. Sheffield. Side bents. 10″ (260 mm). LH grips.

Tailors' Shears. Sheffield. Side bents. 12″ (305 mm). LH grips.

Kitchen Scissor. Sheffield. All-metal with coated grips (yellow, blue or orange). Lower blade serrated. Fully LH.

Hairdressers' Scissor. From Solingen. Fully LH. 5½" (145 mm).

Nursing Scissor. All-metal. Blunt-on-blunt. Rounded ends. Fully LH. 5" (125 mm).

Wallpaper Hangers' Scissor. Fully LH. Extra-long cutting blade. Plastic moulded grips. 10½" (270 mm).

Pens

Osmiroid 'Oxford' Cartridge Pen. Stoutly made and suitable for school use. Fitted with a Rola nib unless otherwise requested.

Osmiroid 'Oxford' Squeeze fill Pen. As above.

Osmiroid 'Viscount' Pen. Squeeze-fill but converts to cartridge. In Gift pack.

Osmiroid 'Windsor' Pen. Squeeze-fill but converts to cartridge. In Gift pack

The Osmiroid range of nibs:

> Rola medium
> Italic medium LH
> Italic Oblique Fine
> Italic Oblique Medium
> Italic Oblique Broad
> B2
> B3
> B4

Osmiroid Lettering Sets for LH writers. Each comes with an Oxford squeeze-fill pen and instruction leaflet:

> Basic Italic. With 3 different nibs.
> Master Italic. With 6 different nibs.
> Basic Calligraphy. With 3 different nibs.
> Master Calligraphy. With 6 different nibs.
> Master Calligraphy De Luxe Set. With six different nibs and high-grade stationery.

Cartridges. For all Osmiroid Pens. Box of 10. Blue or Black.

Osmiroid Dip Pen. With fine or medium LH Italic nib.

Platignum Hooded Pen. With medium LH nib and 4 cartridges.

Platignum Lettering Set. With squeeze-fill Pen and six different LH nibs.

Pelikano Pen. The famous German cartridge pen made specially for LH. This pen delivers ink whether the writer is pulling or pushing. A great boon for the prolific writer.

Pelikano cartridges. Boxes of 6. Blue or Black.

Mitchell Round Hand Pen Set. Dip Pen plus ten different nibs.

Mitchell Italic Pen Set. As above for specialist italic writing. Dip pen + 10 nibs.

Stationery

Index book with LH index insetting 7″ × 5″. About 100 pages. (Set out reverse way round for ease of use by left-hander.) Also 6″ × 4″.

Address book with left-hand index insetting 4½″ × 2″ in red/blue/black with gilt edging, gold-blocked.

Address book with left-hand inset index. Each page ruled for names and addresses. Size 7″ × 3½″. Red/blue/ black, gold-blocked 'You've a right to be left'.

Greetings cards specially designed for greetings to or from a left-hander. Supplied with envelopes.

LH Sir Walter Raleigh colophon, assorted five colours, 4¾″ × 3¾″. Bears the caption 'A left-handed greeting'.

The famous LH dialect names card. 8″ × 3½″. Red/blue/ green.

Birthday card, 'You've a right to be left'. Red/blue/green.

Greetings Card. Featuring Leonardo da Vinci – the most

famous left-hander of them all. Just imagine the Mona Lisa winking?

Playing cards. The numbers are marked on all four corners, thus they may be seen whichever way they are fanned. Red or blue.

Left-hand ruler, inches and centimetres reading from R to L. Perspex. 12″ (300 mm) or 6″ (150 mm).

Left-hand ruler, inches and centimetres, reading from R to L. Plastic. 12″ (300 mm).

Left-hand ruler, inches and centimetres printed on aluminium. 12″ (300 mm).

T-square, 36″ mahogany. Fully LH.

Posters. Enlargements of Michael Barsley originals. 18″ × 13″. a. You've a right to be left. b. The opening shot in the dextro-sinistral war. c. The superior diner.

Garden and Farm Tools

Pruning Shear by Felco. This famous Swiss-made tool now fully LH.

Pruning shear by Leyat. Swiss-made. Fully LH.

Sickle. A very sharp and handy tool from Germany. 15″. Fully LH.

Grass Edge Trimmer. A very handy tool for trimming the edge of your lawn with the left hand.

Pottery and Hand-thrown Stoneware

Craftsman-designed pots.

Pitchers, Casseroles, Mixing bowls, Oil & vinegar bottles. Moustache cup. Decorated glaze finish stoneware. Each individually decorated.

Miscellany

Sailmarkers' Palm. Fully LH. Suitable for all types of heavy sewing.

Farriers' Knife. Sheffield steel with horn handle. Fully LH.

Clasp Knife. Single blade folding into a substantial handle thus providing a firm grip. Sheffield. Blade 3½". Blade 2¾".

Corn Plane. The design of the blade makes it a handy pedicure implement for the LH.

Boomerang. Superbly made. Fully LH and very accurate. 'Champion', 30". 'Junior', 24".

T-shirts. Top-quality non-shrink cotton. With a design and slogan 'I've a right to be left-handed'. White/red/yellow/blue. Size 1 (30"), Size 2 (32"), Size 3 (36"), Size 4, (40") Size 5 (44"). Child's. Size 26" or 28".

Badge. 2¼" diameter with pin. With design and slogan 'I've a right to be left-handed'. Pink/yellow/blue/purple/white.

Key ring. 2⅛" diameter. Design and slogan 'I've a right to be left' and mirror-backed.

Keytainer. Holds 5 keys in suede or leather.

The Moppit Glove. Just slip your hand into the Moppit glove and dust your objets d'art, etc. A special preparation removes all dust and polishes. Glamorous and practical.

Books

Lefthanded; Righthanded by Mark Brown. Hardback, cloth bound. Informative and amusing. 140 pages.

Lefthanded Calligraphy by Vance Studley. A very clear and well-illustrated exposition. 64 pages.

Left Hand Guitar Book. For beginners.

Helping your left-handed child to write. Reprint from WHERE magazine with simple instructions and diagrams. For parents and teachers.

Teaching left-handed children by Margaret Clark. A great help to parents and teachers.

Left-handed knitting by Regina Hurlburt. A long-awaited textbook. Fully illustrated.

Left-handed needlepoint by Regina Hurlburt. An expert left-handed needlewoman has set down in simple language how she taught her left-handed daughter.

Left-handed Crochet by Regina Hurlburt. A further excellent textbook from this brilliant expert.

Index

Sports and activities handbooks – in paperback from Grafton Books

Pat Davis
Badminton Complete (illustrated)   £1.25   ☐

Bruce Tegner
Karate (illustrated)   £1.50   ☐

Bruce Tulloh
The Complete Distance Runner (illustrated)   £1.95   ☐

Meda Mander
How to Trace Your Ancestors (illustrated)   £1.50   ☐

Tom Hopkins
How to Master the Art of Selling   £3.50   ☐

William Prentice
How to Start a Successful Business   £2.95   ☐

Susan Glascock
A Woman's Guide to Starting Her Own Business   £2.50   ☐

Gyles Brandreth
The Complete Puzzler   £1.50   ☐

Patrick Duncan (Editor)
The Panther Crossword Compendium (Vols 1 and 2)   £1.95   ☐
                                                                each
Quizwords 1   £1.50   ☐
Quizwords 2   £1.50   ☐

Peter Wheeler
Rugby from the Front (illustrated)   £1.95   ☐

To order direct from the publisher just tick the titles you want
and fill in the order form.

Health and self-help books – in paperback from Grafton Books

W H Bates		
Better Eyesight Without Glasses	£2.50	☐
Laurence E Morehouse and Leonard Gross		
Total Fitness	£2.50	☐
Constance Mellor		
Guide to Natural Health	£1.25	☐
Natural Remedies for Common Ailments	£1.95	☐
Sonya Richmond		
Yoga and Your Health	£1.25	☐
Phyllis Speight		
Homoeopathy	£1.50	☐
Dr Richard B Stuart		
Act Thin, Stay Thin	£1.50	☐
Dr Carl C Pfeiffer and Jane Banks		
Total Nutrition	£1.50	☐
Dr Hamilton Hall		
Be Your Own Back Doctor	£2.50	☐
José Silva and Michael Miele		
The Silva Mind Control Method	£2.95	☐
Geneen Roth		
Breaking Free from Compulsive Eating	£2.95	☐
Feeding the Hungry Heart	£2.50	☐

To order direct from the publisher just tick the titles you want and fill in the order form.

All these books are available at your local bookshop or newsagent, or can be ordered direct from the publisher.

To order direct from the publishers just tick the titles you want and fill in the form below.

Name _____

Address _____

_____

Send to:
Grafton Cash Sales
PO Box 11, Falmouth, Cornwall TR10 9EN.

Please enclose remittance to the value of the cover price plus:

UK 60p for the first book, 25p for the second book plus 15p per copy for each additional book ordered to a maximum charge of £1.90.

BFPO 60p for the first book, 25p for the second book plus 15p per copy for the next 7 books, thereafter 9p per book.

Overseas including Eire £1.25 for the first book, 75p for second book and 28p for each additional book.

Grafton Books reserve the right to show new retail prices on covers, which may differ from those previously advertised in the text or elsewhere.